Container Gardening
for Beginners

The Complete Guide to Growing Your Own
Vegetables, Fruits, Herbs, and Flowers
in Pots, Tubs, and Grow Bags

Max Barnes

Your Free Gift

I'd like to offer you a gift as a way of saying thank you for purchasing this book. It's the eBook called 5 Easy Ways to Preserve Your Harvest. Sooner or later, you'll reach a point where you're able to grow more vegetables and fruits than you can eat, so I've created this book to help you preserve your harvest so that you could enjoy it later. You can get your free eBook by scanning the QR code below with your phone. Alternatively, please send me an email to maxbarnesbooks@gmail.com and I will send you the free book.

SPECIAL BONUS!
Want this book for free?

Get FREE unlimited access to it and all of
my new books by joining our community!

**Scan with
your camera
to join!**

Garden Planner, Journal and Log Book

Keeping a journal to keep track of your garden and plants can help you determine what worked well and what didn't so that you can repeat your successes and avoid mistakes in the future. To help you plan your garden as well as keep all the important information about your garden and plants in one convenient place in an organized manner, I've created a garden planner, journal, and log book. Please scan the QR code below to find out more. Alternatively, please send me an email to maxbarnesbooks@gmail.com and I will send you the link to the journal.

  **Scan with your camera to find out more**

Contents

Introduction

There are so many incredible benefits to container gardening! Container gardening is easy to do even for people who are new to gardening. With container gardening, you can grow vegetables, fruits, herbs, and flowers even if you have limited space. You can control the quality of the soil, so if you have moved to an area with poor soil quality that restricts the type of plants you're able to grow, container gardening is a great way around this. You can move your garden around easily. If you move home, you can take your plants with you. If you live in a city area and don't have much space, container gardening is ideal for you.

Many people would like to grow their own vegetables, fruits, herbs, and flowers at home, but they don't know where to start, and often think that they are unable to do this because they don't have a garden, a greenhouse or a polytunnel, and lots of space. A lot of people have heard about container gardening, but if they're new to it, they can feel overwhelmed or think it's too complicated for them. Some of the reasons for thinking it's complicated may be due to a lack of knowledge on the subject, a distrust of Internet sources, and the difficulty of knowing whether the information is accurate and high quality.

This book is thoroughly researched as well as based on sound and successful experience, and it will save you hundreds of hours of time trying to do the research yourself, having all the information you need in one convenient place. *Container Gardening for Beginners* will teach you everything you need to know in order to start and maintain your own container garden and grow your own vegetables, fruits, herbs, and flowers in containers. This book will teach you everything you need to know about container gardening, including choosing the right containers for your plants, creating the perfect growing medium, starting and maintaining your container garden, and dealing with pests and diseases.

What This Book Will Cover

Here's a short overview of what this book will cover:

- This book will outline the many benefits of container gardening, explaining what can be grown in containers and how to be successful at this, plus giving you information on the tools and equipment you will require.

- After reading this book, you will know how to choose the right container for your plants.

- You will learn how to find the best location for your container garden so that the plants can thrive and produce an abundance of produce.

- This book will explain how to create the perfect growing medium for your plants to grow in, how to mix potting soil, and how to test your soil.

- You will learn how to start seeds and cuttings and plant seedlings to start off a container garden.

- You will learn how to maintain your garden, how often it should be watered, and how best to care for your plants at different growth stages.

- Should your plants experience any pests, there is a chapter in this book that will help you learn how to identify them and how to deal with them.

- This book will let you know the best time to harvest your vegetables, fruits, and herbs and provide information on how to store them.

- Finally, this book ends with plant profiles that contain detailed information on how to grow various vegetables, fruits, herbs, and flowers. This is intended as a useful reference resource for you to refer back to when required.

Why I'm Writing This Book

My name is Max. I grew up on a farm, and helping my grandmother Anna in her garden is one of my earliest memories. She was very innovative and ahead of her time and regularly experimented with different gardening methods. I have continued to do this growing up. Most of the plants we eat are grown on my property using different methods, including container gardening.

Container gardening helps me lead a sustainable lifestyle, and I love this! I adore the fact that I have control over what we eat and can grow my own food from seed right to the lovely, fresh, delicious-tasting produce. When I go out into our garden late afternoon with baskets to harvest our produce, it is truly one of the happiest parts of my day. I love harvesting fresh vegetables, fruits, and herbs that we've grown and seeing their vibrant colors, knowing how juicy, tasty, and flavorsome they're going to be in meals, and planning what different meals we can cook with them. We grow so much produce we have to be inventive with pickles, jams, chutneys, and baked goods. When I pick baskets of vegetables, fruits, and berries, I'm instantly transported back to being a child and memories of doing the very same with my grandmother Anna. She was the one who taught me everything I learned about gardening methods, giving me the skills that I need to grow a variety of different seasonal plants all year round.

My grandmother taught me specifically about growing plants in containers, and all throughout my life I have built upon the foundations of what she taught me and have kept learning and honing my skills so that I get better results. I have learned lots of helpful tips and tricks over the years, and I've learned from when things went wrong. I'm sharing decades of my experience in this book to save you from making the same mistakes that I did. I'm hoping that you get the benefits quicker with fewer headaches than I did.

My purpose for writing this book is that I would like to tell everyone just how easy it is to grow plants in containers and that the benefits of doing so far outweigh the time, money, and effort invested. This is not a complicated process. It's not that expensive to do, and it's not that time-consuming. But ultimately, you end up with an abundance of lovely, fresh produce! You know exactly how it has been grown (without pesticides or chemicals if you have chosen to grow organically). It hasn't been transported through a long supply chain—from farms to warehouses, to supermarkets, and then to your home—it's already at your home. You don't have to use fuel to drive to a supermarket to purchase it. Growing your own produce is often cheaper than buying items from a supermarket, and the best thing about growing your own food is that you know exactly how it has been grown. You will undoubtedly get more produce than you and your family

can use, so you may end up making pickles, chutneys, or jams to preserve some of it. You may sell some of your produce locally or give it away to friends, family, or community places that make food affordable or free to those struggling.

This book is a detailed guide aimed at beginners to container gardening, and it will give you step-by-step instructions on how to start and maintain a container garden and grow vegetables, fruits, herbs, and flowers in containers. It is not a guide to anything else outside the realm of container gardening.

So, without further ado, let's get started on the exciting journey of container gardening and move onto the very first chapter that will give you information regarding the benefits of growing in containers and a general outline as to some of the types of plants you could decide to grow in containers.

Chapter 1: Why Grow in Containers?

You clearly have an interest in growing plants in containers if you have purchased this book. But if you had any niggling doubts about whether this is a good idea, whether you would be successful, whether it's worth the time and money invested, and how difficult it may be, I hope that by the end (and maybe just part way through) of this chapter they will have vanished as you're empowered and enthused by the many more benefits of container gardening!

I am thrilled with all the plants we grow and all the beautiful vegetables, fruits, and herbs we harvest from our container garden. From succulent bell peppers and chili peppers to tasty tomatoes, sweet strawberries, comforting potatoes, fresh salad, fragrant herbs, tangy cucamelons, delicious squash, crisp green beans, and much more.

This chapter will cover the benefits and drawbacks of container gardening, what you can grow in containers, principles for successful container gardening, and the tools and equipment you need for container gardening.

Benefits and Drawbacks of Container Gardening

Benefits

1. **No space constraints**

One of the best things about container gardening is that you do not need access to acres of land, fields, a large garden, or to live in the countryside in order to grow vegetables, fruits, and herbs. You can start a container garden in a relatively small space, such as a yard, a small balcony, or a porch. You can put the containers on the ground, attach them to windowsills or walls, or hang them at the entrance of your home.

2. **Appearance**

Container gardens have the ability to make the place where you live look more beautiful and smell incredible too, with herbs and some flowers. I don't think there's anything more beautiful than lots of natural green leaves and vibrant vegetables and fruits growing. It adds a beautiful splash of color, a wonderful fragrance, and you can choose what type, style, and size of containers you want to use, whether you'd like a uniform color and style or opt for a more bohemian look. We personally have containers of all shapes, sizes, colors, and patterns, and we love how vibrant this looks. People often kindly purchase containers for us for birthday or Christmas presents, and they're always highly valued by us, and knowing it was a gift adds sentimental feeling to that container and the plants we grow in it.

3. Portability

You can easily move plants in containers. So, if you decide that there's a better location in your garden for them, you can move them. If you decide that the weather is too cold and frosty for them, you can bring the containers indoors. If you move house, you can take all the plants that you've lovingly grown with you easily without worrying that they could be damaged and traumatized with the move. That can be an issue with garden plants—you won't be able to move them as easily.

4. Poor garden soil quality—no problem

If you don't have good soil where you live, perhaps it is very dry, clay-like, boggy, or lacking nutrients, then this isn't an issue with container gardening. You can purchase potting soil or potting mix from garden centers, or you can mix potting soil yourself and fill the containers with exactly the right type of soil that your plants need. Some plants will want more acidic soil, some more alkaline, depending on what plants you're growing.

5. Fewer weeds

Personally, I think this is a great benefit—you won't have to weed very often at all compared to a regular garden. If you have a garden where you're fed up with having to weed, starting a container garden can help you avoid having to weed often.

6. No heavy manual labor

Unlike an in-ground garden that may need digging and tilling (unless you opt for no-dig gardening method) as well as regular weeding, there is no heavy manual labor with container gardening, which can make it quite accessible to a large number of people. Because containers are higher and you can place them on raised areas, you don't even have to bend down so far to tend to the containers as you would with plants in the ground. You won't require any large or heavy gardening tools, just light hand-held tools, water, and fertilizer.

Drawbacks

1. Need to water often

Plants in containers dry out quickly, even if they're outside where it rains, so you will need to water them regularly.

2. Need to fertilize frequently

Because you can't use compost and mulch in container gardens as easily as in a normal garden, you will have to use fertilizer frequently.

3. Vulnerability to cold

Container plants can be a bit more vulnerable to cold and frost, so you might have to move your container plants somewhere warmer if the weather starts getting cold.

4. Containers can limit growth

Obviously, in an in-ground garden, plants' roots have the ability to go down into the ground and spread out in all directions much further. But in a container, they're contained (pardon the pun). This can limit the growth of plants and mean that they can be more stunted than they would be in an in-ground garden.

Personally, I don't view these drawbacks as significant things that would put me off container gardening, and most of them apply to traditional gardening as well. With a traditional garden, you need to water and fertilize your plants to keep them in good health and try to protect them from cold and frost too. But it's worth being aware of these drawbacks before starting a container garden so that you can make an informed decision whether container gardening suits you. Regarding containers limiting growth, you can minimize it by choosing the right container for your plants. The next chapter will cover which containers are best for which type of plants so that your plants can thrive and produce an abundance of produce for you. Also, Chapter 9 has information on what size containers you need for different plants.

What Can You Grow in Containers?

You can grow almost any plant you can think of in containers. But you may require a massive container and a place to put it for some plants. But realistically, some plants will do better than others, and some plants would thrive better in the ground, mostly because they're able to spread their root system out.

Best Plants to Grow in Containers

Vegetables that grow especially well in containers include tomatoes, cucumbers, peppers, onions, lettuce, spinach, kale, Swiss chard, beans, peas, carrots, potatoes, beets, pumpkins, eggplants, and zucchini.

Fruits include strawberries, blueberries, gooseberries, and various fruits trees, such as lemon, apple, cherry, fig, and peach trees. You can get dwarf varieties of many fruit trees.

Most herbs grow well in containers, including basil, mint, chives, rosemary, oregano, parsley, coriander, and thyme.

You may want an injection of color in your garden with flowers. Geraniums, marigolds, begonias, coleus, scarlet sage, and flowering tobacco grow well in containers and will look good all throughout the summer. Other plants and shrubs will last forever, such as hostas, ferns, lavender, sedums, grasses, and dwarf conifers.

Principles for Successful Container Gardening

Container Size

The size of the container needs to suit the plant. A good example of this is that you can't grow tomatoes in a small pot. They need space to grow, and you'll need to put stakes in the pot to support them as they grow. Garlic, however, shouldn't be put in a large container because garlic has a short root system and likes being in a small container. Container size will be discussed in more detail in the next chapter of this book, and Chapter 9 has container size requirements for many different plants.

Use Potting Soil or Potting Mix

When growing plants in containers, you need to pay special attention to the soil you use. Soil taken from your yard or garden is too dense to use in a pot. It can also have pests and diseases. Instead, use potting soil or potting mix for your container garden.

Good Drainage

It is essential that containers have drainage holes because otherwise roots of plants would rot, and plants will die. You can put paper towels or newspaper over drainage holes in the base of pots before filling them with potting soil to prevent the soil from washing out.

Fertilizer

You need to fertilize your plants so that they grow and thrive. Because containers dry out much quicker than plants in the garden, you will need to water them more often. As you water them, you will wash out the nutrients, so you will need to fertilize them regularly.

Light-Colored Containers

If you use light-colored containers, they will absorb less heat than dark-colored ones. They won't get as hot throughout the summer, so they won't dry out as easily and will keep your plants' roots cool.

Position Containers Before Filling

We have made this mistake more than once. But it's very easy to forget just how heavy a container can be once it's filled with soil and plants. It's always advisable to find the perfect position for a container in your garden before you start to fill it with soil and plant it up. Depending on what your plants need, look for places in your garden that have sun and shade accordingly.

Mulch Large Containers

You can put a layer of mulch on the top of large containers to help keep soil cool and keep moisture in, but try to keep mulch away from plant stems.

Light for Indoor Container Plants

If you have placed container plants inside during the colder winter months, try to ensure they have plenty of sunlight to allow them to grow well. You can use grow lights if your plants don't get enough sunlight.

General Welfare

As mentioned previously, you will need to water and fertilize your container plants regularly. You will also want to ensure that all your plants in containers look the best they are able to. Chapter 6 of this book will look at maintaining your garden, but to summarize some of the key points here, you will need to prune and deadhead plants to get rid of dead flowers and dead or overgrown stems or branches. If plants have grown too tall (leggy) and aren't blooming, you'll need to cut them down. You'll have to take out any plants that are dead or not doing well and replace them with new plants. Most importantly, you'll need to check your plants for pests and any signs of diseases regularly. Chapter 7 will cover dealing with pests and diseases.

Thriller, Spiller, and Filler

If you are planting flowers in your containers for an injection of color and beautiful scents, I'd suggest planting a thriller, a spiller, and a filler. A thriller is a plant that is the focal point of your container—this could be coleus or geranium. A spiller is a plant that will spill over the edge of the pot and hang down—it could be creeping zinnia, petunia, or ornamental sweet potatoes. Fillers are plants that tend to have smaller leaves and flowers, and these add color and fill in the gaps in the arrangement throughout the growing season. Good fillers include ornamental peppers, begonias, verbenas, and salvias. You may decide to add plants to give the display more height, such as purple fountain grass, or place a trellis at the back of the container that you could add a vine to so that it will climb up and give the display height.

Tools and Equipment for Container Gardening

What's great about container gardening is that you don't need any of the heavy-duty, weighty tools that you require for normal gardening. You don't need a rake, a spade, or a pitchfork. You will, however, need some hand tools that will be covered in more detail below.

You have an enormous amount of choice regarding the different containers you could purchase for your container garden and the plants you could grow. This is why it's such an incredibly varied hobby that can appeal to a lot of different people.

You will definitely need the following tools and equipment for your container garden:

- Containers

- A watering can—if you buy one with a long spout, this will help you water the back of containers too.

- Potting soil or potting mix

- Compost (This is optional, but adding compost at the time of planting will enrich your potting soil with nutrients, improve its structure and texture, and will also help retain moisture.)

- Fertilizer

- Secateurs—these are needed for pruning and training plants and shrubs and also for cutting herbs and flowers. Parrot secateurs with a cross beak are a popular type.

- Hand fork—this is useful for loosening compacted soil and can be used for weeding too.

- Hand trowel—this will come in useful for planting and weeding. Ideally, purchase a stainless steel one. Narrow trowels are good for digging deep and narrow holes without disturbing nearby plants.

- Dibber—this is a useful tool for making small holes for seeds and seedlings.

- Hand rake—this little rake is great for weeding, light cultivation, leveling soil, and adding soil amendments.

- Hand shears—these are for larger plants that you'll need to trim back in the summer or fall months.

- Garden knife—it is a useful tool for transplanting, cutting sod, and dividing plants.

- Pruning knife and saw—this isn't an essential bit of kit, and you may only require this if you have very large branches that you can't cut with secateurs.

- Spray bottle—used for misting plants that need this and also for mixing up pesticide solutions to spray your plants with if you have a pest infestation.

- Gardening gloves—to stop your hands from getting messy, dry, or stabbed with thorns.

- There are other little bits and pieces that you may need, such as gardening wire, ties, a hammer, ring eyes, screws, and nails for a wire frame.

Container gardening takes some time and effort, but it's so rewarding to see your plants grow and produce an abundance of wonderful produce! I love planting plants, watering and fertilizing them, and watching them grow. Personally, I think this work is 100% worth it, especially when I see all the fresh, beautiful, home-grown vegetables, fruits, and herbs that I've grown from seed to harvest. Even after all this time, there is still something special about taking a basket out to the garden, picking fresh food, and creating a wholesome meal for the family out of things I have personally grown.

I love the fact that the garden looks stunning with its array of brightly colored and patterned pots and a huge variety of beautiful, colorful vegetables, fruits, herbs, and flowers growing in them. They look and smell fabulous, and everyone who visits comments on how nice they look and smell. Having these beautiful plants in containers makes me want to spend more time outdoors. In the summer months, I often sit outside for a morning cup of tea, and late in the evening too to relax after a day of hard work. It's a beautiful haven to be surrounded by.

Key takeaways from this chapter:

1. The main benefit of container gardening is that it can be done in virtually any space. You can make use of walls, windowsills, and hanging baskets. You can place containers on decking, balconies, and rooftops. They'll make your home look vibrant and attractive. You can easily move most containers to change the appearance of your garden or take them with you if you move. If you have poor soil in your garden—that's not a problem. You can purchase potting soil or potting mix to put in your containers. There are fewer weeds with container gardening than with traditional gardening. And finally, there isn't much heavy manual labor with container gardening.

2. The main drawback of container gardening is that you have to water your containers regularly to stop them from drying out. You will also need to fertilize them often. They will need protecting from the cold. Containers can limit the growth of plants because the roots are contained. But personally, I consider these drawbacks fairly minor and most of them apply to traditional gardening as well.

3. You can grow vegetables, fruits, herbs, and flowers in containers. Vegetables that grow well in containers include tomatoes, peppers, cucumbers, beans, carrots, peas, leafy greens, zucchini, and pumpkins. Herbs, such as basil, chives, rosemary, and thyme, grow well in containers. Fruits that grow well in containers include blueberries, figs, gooseberries, peaches, apples, and strawberries. You can grow flowers in containers too, such as marigolds, geraniums, and begonias.

4. Tips for success with container gardening include having good drainage, fertilizing often, having light-colored containers so that they don't overheat, using good-quality potting soil or potting mix, ensuring plants have lots of light if you move them indoors during the colder months, and ensuring you have a suitable container size for your plants. You can also use the "thriller, spiller, and filler" technique when planning, ensuring you have something attractive that draws the eye, something that flows over the edge of the pot, and plants that grow in abundance to fill in all the gaps. It's a really good idea to put containers in place before you fill them with soil because they'll be very heavy when they're filled. You can mulch the top of large containers. You will need to look after the container plants' general welfare, which includes watering and fertilizing your plants, pruning and deadheading them, and checking them for pests and any signs of diseases regularly.

5. Regarding container gardening tools, there is a wide variety you can purchase, and you'll probably pick these up as you go along as you require them. Some of the more essential ones include containers, potting soil or potting mix, a watering can, fertilizer, a hand trowel, and gardening gloves.

The next chapter will look at how to choose the right containers for your plants, looking at the different types of containers available and the advantages and disadvantages of each type.

Chapter 2: Choosing Containers for Your Plants

Now that you've read Chapter 1, and hopefully you're convinced of the many benefits of container gardening, you may now be interested in what containers you should choose for your plants. So, this chapter will cover in detail different container types and how to choose the right containers for your plants.

The size of containers is important to think about when you start a container garden. It is easier to grow plants in larger containers rather than smaller ones. Large containers have more soil in them, which helps with water retention. Small containers dry out very quickly. In general, with containers, you will find that you need to water them more often than plants in the ground.

Often the containers for your container garden are the largest investment you'll make. I would suggest going for better containers that will last for years.

You can, of course, also be really creative with the containers you use, and this can be part of the fun. I've seen people use all sorts of things as containers, from an old toilet bowl to buckets, baskets, boots, and urns. Provided you can make drainage holes in the containers and pick suitable plants for them, you have a great deal of options.

Types of Containers

As mentioned previously, you'll find it easier to grow plants in larger containers rather than smaller ones because you can fit more soil in a larger container, and it will stay moist for longer. Things like hanging baskets can dry out quickly, and on a really hot summer day you may need to water them twice to ensure your plants are kept healthy.

If you're doing mixed planting, the container needs to be big enough for all the plants to have space to grow. Using light-colored containers will help keep the soil cooler. Dark containers absorb more heat and they absorb it quicker.

The only limits to the size and weight of containers are down to the space and support constraints that you have. If you're placing containers on a balcony, decking, or a roof, check that these are study and will support the weight safely.

Drainage holes in containers are essential because plants would get waterlogged without proper drainage and die eventually because the roots will rot, so it's essential that there are enough holes for water to drain out. If you have a container without drainage holes, you can either carefully drill holes in it, or you could use this type of pot as an outer cover (cachepot) to be decorative. Ideally, you should have four or five ½-inch (1.2 cm) holes in a 5-gallon (19L) container. If your container is inside, then you'll need something under your container to catch the drained water and prevent it from damaging your floors.

You can get self-watering containers, double-walled containers, hanging baskets, and window boxes, which can be a nice option for smaller plants that you need to water often. You may decide to repurpose old wood. Or you may decide to use buckets—5-gallon (19L) buckets for containers are perhaps the smallest you'd want them to be. If you have a limited budget, you could look to see if anyone has any containers available for free on websites like Freecycle.

There are many different types of containers that you could choose to have in your container garden, and each container type has its advantages and disadvantages. Different container types as well as their advantages and disadvantages will be covered below.

Clay or Terracotta Containers

These are probably my personal favorite type of container. They look so beautiful, but they can break easily and can be damaged by frosts, snow, and thawing out. Their main advantage is that they are porous, so air can get in and water can evaporate. However, if the terracotta itself is dry, it can leach water from soil, leaving it dry. They're also not really suited for plants such as hardy perennials or shrubs that will be outdoors all year round. They come in a wide range of colors, from pale to orange-brown. Many clay pots are covered with a beautiful glaze. These are a bit more durable and will keep moisture in better than non-glazed pots. They can be quite heavy and can chip or crack.

Cast Concrete or Stone Containers

These are really long lasting and come in a variety of shapes and sizes, and the good thing about them is that you can leave them outdoors all year round. Because of their weight, they also won't tip or blow over easily. They are heavy, though, so moving them to different locations won't be easy. They are also probably too heavy for decking and most balconies. It could be an advantage, though, depending on the area that you live in. Because they're so heavy (or fixed permanently), it would prevent thieves from stealing your prized pots or plants.

You can purchase containers that are concrete mixed with other things, like fiberglass (this mix is sometimes called fiberstone), vermiculite, or perlite, which can make them much lighter. Having small shrubs or trees in containers like these is ideal.

Plastic and Fiberglass Containers

Plastic and fiberglass containers are quite light, and they're not too expensive to buy. They come in a wide variety of shapes and sizes. It is best to choose sturdy and flexible containers because thin and stiff plastic or fiberglass containers will crack easily when it's cold or break with time. They are lightweight, durable, and quite resistant to most types of weather. If you live in a windy location, you may find that they blow over frequently.

Polyurethane Foam Containers

These are very light containers—they weigh 90% less than terracotta ones, but they are made to look like terracotta. They are good because they don't chip or crack easily. They also help keep plants' roots protected from extreme temperatures, whether that's hot or cold. These are a good option for plants that stay out all year round.

Wooden Containers

We have some lovely wooden containers in our garden. We have a big wooden trough that we initially used as an herb garden (it now has flowers in it) that we made out of wooden pallets and painted the outside. It has lasted for over 5 years so far. We also use wine barrels as containers. Wood looks beautiful and natural, and it will protect the roots of your plants from extreme temperatures.

Certain types of wood will be less prone to rotting, such as cedar, redwood, or locust. Never put creosote on wooden containers because it's toxic to plants. Never place edible plants into a wooden container that has been treated because chemicals from treated wood may get into the plants. To help with moisture retention, you can line some wooden containers or put another container inside them. Many people line their wooden containers with plastic. Landscape fabric is also good for lining wooden containers. If you have bought wooden containers, check that they are well constructed because wood will shrink when it's cold and expand when it's hot.

Metal Containers

The main benefit of these is that they're strong. Cast iron containers will last forever. They are heavy and won't blow over in the wind. You can also get sheet metal containers made from tin, copper, steel, or aluminum.

They're not easy to move around because of their weight and may be too heavy for decking or balconies. Metal containers can also overheat your plants' roots in the summer. If you think of a metal utensil, such as a spoon in a saucepan when you're cooking and how hot that gets, consider that when the sun is beating down on the metal, it too will warm up and heat up the soil and plants' roots inside it. You also run the risk of metal rusting. We have one metal container that we inherited when we moved in, but we keep it in a very shaded area of our garden.

Grow Bags

Grow bags are becoming a popular alternative to other types of containers. They offer some advantages over terracotta or plastic pots. They are lightweight and therefore easier to move around. They breathe and drain well, and they help keep soil cool in the summer. They can help prevent plants from becoming root bound. When roots reach the side of a grow bag, they come in contact with drier soil and more air and stop growing—this is called air pruning. In other types of containers, roots would circle the pot and the plant would eventually become root bound.

They do dry out pretty quickly, quicker than other types of containers. To remedy this, you can add plastic bottle drip irrigation, a terracotta olla, or even get a grow bag with a reservoir (self-watering grow bag).

Grow bags come in various sizes: 5 gallons (19L), 10 gallons (38L), 15 gallons (57L), 20 gallons (76L), and so on. They are usually made of felt or other non-woven, pressed fabrics. I'd suggest getting polypropylene felt-like fabric grow bags. They are breathable and allow air pruning.

Hanging Baskets

These can be made from many different materials, including solid plastic ones with water reservoirs, woven wicker baskets for a more earthy, homemade feel, and wire-framed ones for a more modern touch. The key thing to keep in mind with hanging baskets is that they dry out really quickly, so you will need to water these regularly, especially on hot summer days. Like with other types of containers, the size of a hanging basket is important. If a basket is too small for your plants, you will need to water and prune your plants regularly. Generally, the bigger the basket, the better. A bigger basket can retain more moisture, which means you won't have to water it as often.

The lining of the basket is really important. You can have hanging baskets lined with fibrous material, such as sphagnum moss, cocoa liner, burlap liner, or supamoss.

Sphagnum moss holds in moisture really well because of its thick, lush texture and largely dry and empty cells. It's also naturally free from bugs and pests. It looks really nice in a basket, but it can be tedious to work with.

Cocoa liners are usually sold pre-molded to fit certain size baskets. They look really tidy. They are pretty thick, however, which makes them unsuitable for planting on the sides, so if you're going for a more rustic look, it's best to look elsewhere.

Burlap liners are inexpensive, and the material is flexible and environmentally friendly. The main drawback of this material is that it retains almost no water because it's treated with copper to slow the degradation process.

Supamoss is perhaps the most versatile liner for a hanging basket. It's filled with holes and has excellent drainage, but it doesn't dry out too quickly because of the thick plastic coating that helps retain enough water for your plants. It looks natural, even though it's the most artificial material of the four mentioned. This liner is also malleable, so you can adjust it to suit your plants.

Choosing the Right Pot for Every Plant

The type of plants you intend to grow will determine what size the containers need to be. There are 6 key considerations when determining the correct pot for your plants:

1. What is the root system of the plant like? How large will it be? What sort of shape is it?

2. Is the plant you want to grow an annual (completes its life cycle in one growing season) or a perennial (lives more than 2 years)?

3. How fast will the plant grow?

4. What will the size of the plant be once it has grown?

5. Can the plant survive in dry conditions?

6. Will you combine plants in the container?

Generally, the bigger the container, the better. The main advantage of having large containers is that they dry out slower than smaller ones. However, tall and narrow pots dry out quicker than short and wide ones. So, unless you have a deep-rooted plant, I'd suggest getting shorter and wider containers.

One tip for choosing the correct size of a container is that you should pick a container that is 1/3 of the height of the plant, measured from the soil to the highest leaf. This is generally true for above-ground plants, but may not be true for root crops. If you want to grow multiple plants in one container, the container needs to be big enough for all the plants to have space to grow.

If plants' roots do not have enough room, plants can become root bound, and they won't thrive. If you have small containers, then you can consider growing dwarf and compact cultivars. You can get dwarf or bush forms of tomatoes, pumpkins, and winter squash.

Most plants won't thrive in standing water, so it's important that your containers have a drainage hole at the bottom. If you want to use a container without drainage holes for decorative purposes, you can use it as a cachepot that holds the pot the plant is growing in. This technique is known as double potting. A cachepot doesn't need drainage holes, and it should be large enough to accommodate a saucer that fits the growing pot.

In Chapter 3, we'll move on to looking at the perfect location for your container garden, but you do need to give some thought whether the plants you intend to put in containers will be in the sun all day because containers dry out quickly, especially terracotta pots and hanging baskets. Also, remember that dark-colored containers absorb heat and dry out faster than light-colored ones. If someone isn't available to water your containers every day, you may have to consider a drip tray or a reservoir to help keep your plants watered.

If you plan to leave a container outside all year round, then you'd be better off with frost-safe containers made from wood, cement, or stone. Fiberglass and resin containers can also be left outside in the winter. Some plastic pots can survive the winter fine but will become brittle over time. If you think you'll need to move your containers around a lot, then they need to be light so that you can lift them.

These are general considerations for choosing containers for your plants. Chapter 9 will container size requirements for different plants in more detail.

We do have a real mix of containers in our garden, and once you start growing in containers, I can promise you it's really addictive. We have a lot of terracotta containers with different vibrant colors and patterns. We have a wooden trough and wooden barrels. We have some concrete containers and lots of polyurethane foam containers. We have window boxes, hanging baskets, and lots of trellises with vines growing up. We have wonderful plants everywhere you can look, and it looks tremendous.

Key takeaways from this chapter:

1. Larger containers retain moisture better.

2. If you are putting containers on decking, a balcony, or a roof, check that they can support the weight.

3. Ensure containers have drainage holes.

4. Clay containers retain moisture better if they are glazed. The downside of clay containers is that they can be damaged by frosts or thawing out and can crack. They also chip rather easily.

5. Concrete containers are very durable and won't blow over easily. However, they are too heavy for decking or balconies.

6. Plastic or fiberglass containers are the most economical. If you buy these, try to choose sturdier ones because if they're thin, they may crack in cold weather or with age.

7. Wooden containers can be kept outside all year round. Never put creosote on wooden containers because it's toxic to plants. Also, make sure wood hasn't been treated because chemicals from treated wood may get into plants.

8. Metal containers, especially cast iron ones, can last forever, but sheet metal can rust, and they can get really hot in the sun.

9. You can grow dwarf or bush forms of plants in smaller containers.

10. Containers should be 1/3 of the height of plants.

The next chapter will look at choosing the perfect location for your container garden. This may depend on what sun or shade you have on your property, the type of plants you have chosen, and how sheltered this area is from the elements too. The chapter will also cover some garden design essentials.

Chapter 3: Choosing the Perfect Location for Your Garden

This chapter will look at where you can locate your containers so that they look stunning and your plants can grow to their best potential. Specifically, this chapter will look at how to choose the best location for your container garden, weighing up the various options you have available and taking into account sun exposure, water, and accessibility. It will also look at some garden design essentials.

How to Choose the Right Location for Your Container Garden

The location of your container garden is really important because it will determine how much sun your plants get, how much wind they experience, and you need to consider how accessible the garden is for you so that you can easily tend to the plants. You will have to think about how large your containers need to be, and this will determine to some extent how much space your container garden needs to fit these in. It will also depend on what space you have available. Consider the space you have available and work out what options you have.

Space

It can be a sensible idea to measure the length, width, and height of the space you have available for your plants because this will help you work out the number of plants you can fit into the space you have available. Plants need enough space to grow without being too crowded next to one another. It's sensible to consider what vertical space you have too. You could make a note of these measurements in a notebook or on your phone and take this with you when you go to purchase containers and/or plants. Depending on how much space you have available, you can grow climbing cucumbers, squash, and melons using hanging trellises to support them. You can also grow small trees in containers, such as apple, cherry, fig, peach, or citrus trees.

If you are limited for space and perhaps only have a balcony or windowsills, then you could consider trying to utilize all the space you have available by growing plants vertically. You can grow plants up a trellis or using hanging planters.

If you start growing plants in a part of your garden and the plants aren't thriving quite as you expected, the beauty of a container garden is that most containers can be picked up and moved to another location. So, my suggestion would be to do some research on the plant and check how much sunlight it requires, and then see if there's a more suited spot for it in the space you have. If the place where you live has a community space, you could also try moving them there if you're allowed to do that.

Evaluating Sun Requirements and Exposure

All plants require a certain number of hours of daily exposure to sunlight in order to grow and thrive. When you purchase seeds, seedlings, or plants from a nursery, their ideal sunlight requirements are almost always printed on the seed packet, tag, or label. Many vegetables require at least 6 hours of sunlight per day to grow.

If you look at a seed packet or a plant label, you'll find the following terms that describe sun requirements:

- Full sun
- Full sun to partial shade
- Partial shade (or part shade)
- Dappled sun/shade
- Full shade

Full sun means that an area must receive 6–8 hours of direct sunlight on most days mostly between the hours of 10 a.m. and 4 p.m. Many plants need full sun to grow, flower, and produce fruit, but some plants cannot handle the intense heat and/or dry conditions that often come with that much exposure to the sun. You can place a 2–3-inch (5–7.5 cm) layer of mulch to help keep in soil moisture and keep the roots cool (this will be discussed in more detail later in the book). When you choose plants, do some research on the species to determine if there are limitations on their full sun requirement. Plants that are sensitive to heat will usually come with a caution that they require some shelter from direct sunlight in mid-afternoon in hot climates. One way around this is to place these sensitive plants where they receive most of their sunlight in the morning or very late afternoon when temperatures might be cooler. As long as the plants receive at least 6–8 hours of direct sunlight, they should grow well.

The terms "partial (or part) sun" and "partial (or part) shade" are essentially the same and are often used interchangeably. Partial sun or partial shade means that an area must get 4–6 hours of sun exposure per day, preferably in the cooler hours of the morning. There is a subtle difference between these two terms, however. Partial sun puts greater emphasis on plants receiving at least the minimum sun requirements of 4–6 hours. These plants are typically more resistant to heat and need the sunlight to flower and produce fruit, just not as much as plants that need full sun. If they're not flowering or growing up to expectations, you can try moving them to a location that gets more sun. Partial shade means that plants don't tolerate heat as well as plants that need partial sun, and they may need some relief from heat, especially in the afternoon. You can place these plants where there is some shade, for example, near a tree or a fence or on the east side of a structure, which would typically be shaded in the afternoon.

Dappled sun is a rare term, but you might find it used to describe sun requirements of a few plants. Dappled sun is similar to partial shade, but it means the sunlight filters through the branches and foliage of deciduous trees. Deciduous trees shed their leaves annually. Woodland plants, such as trillium, Solomon's seal, and understory trees and shrubs, prefer dappled sun.

Full shade means that plants need 4 hours of sunlight mostly in the morning or late afternoon or a full day of dappled sunlight. Some people think that full shade means no sunlight at all, but that's not true. Very few plants, other than mushrooms, can survive without sunlight.

Direct sunlight means that sunlight is physically hitting the leaves of the plants. Indirect sunlight can mean that the sunlight is going through a window, or is bouncing off walls, or through dappled leaves to reach the plant. If somewhere is classed as shaded, it means that sunlight mostly doesn't reach the plants in this area.

Once you have considered the space you have, you then need to spend some time monitoring which areas of the space receive sun and make notes of how this changes throughout the course of a day. The best way to measure average sunlight exposure is to simply observe the area where you plan to place your containers every hour during the daylight hours over a week or two. Make notes to determine the average amount of sunlight the area receives each hour and where the shadows fall. Make notes whether it's full sun, filtered or dappled light, or full shade.

The path of the sun changes throughout the year, so it's best to measure the light in your garden during the growing season for your plants. You can make a note of how this changes over the seasons so that you're able to select the best plants for your garden.

You can also use flags or stakes to show the light and shadow in your yard. Or you could use some sheets of tracing paper and sketch the yard outline onto each page, then mark where the light and shade is every hour each time using a different sheet of tracing paper, and then you can layer the pages together to get an indication of how much light your yard receives.

If you don't personally have the time to monitor your garden each hour of the day, other options include purchasing a garden light meter, which may also measure moisture in the soil and pH levels too. Or you could take a picture of your garden every hour or set up a time-lapse camera that will do it for you. When you have a sun map, it's much easier to choose suitable plants for your garden by reading seed packets and seeing whether they like full sun, partial sun or shade, or full shade.

When you have determined the average amount of sunlight an area receives, you can choose plants that match the conditions your space has. If you don't have an environment that gets 6–8 hours of sunlight per day, then growing some vegetables may be tough, but you could still grow leafy greens, such as kale, spinach, Swiss chard, mustard greens, and lettuce, and also herbs, such as basil, parsley, mint, rosemary, oregano, thyme, sage, and chives. These leafy greens will give you so many good nutrients and vitamins, and herbs will really give your food a kick of flavor.

If the only space you have is completely in the shade, then you may be able to grow some medicinal plants or houseplants that enjoy the shade.

Shelter from the Elements

Is the area you live in prone to storms and wind? If so, is there anything you could do to put up some protection around the container garden to shelter the plants a little? Plants also don't like extreme heat or cold. If the area you live in is prone to snow, then you may wish to position your plants in a higher part of the garden or on a higher structure so that plants won't get covered in snow.

Water

Think about where you can get water from for your container garden. If you have an outdoor tap or hose—this is ideal, but if you don't, you will have to carry watering cans through other areas of your property. On a previous property, I had to carry water in a watering can through my kitchen, then through a front room, and then out to the garden, and inevitably some water would get splashed on the floor. If you have space, another option you could consider is getting a water butt that collects rainwater for you. Most water butts have a tap that you can then use to fill up watering cans. Rainwater is good and healthy for watering container garden plants, and it's free from chemicals found in tap water.

Accessibility

Your container garden needs to be easily accessible by you because your plants will not survive, let alone thrive, if you can't regularly water and fertilize them, prune off any bits of plants that have died, and generally check their health each day.

Garden Design Essentials

When you're designing your container garden, the key thing is that it brings you joy and happiness. You need to enjoy looking at where you position it, but do be practical too regarding sunlight, water, and accessibility because it's not going to look nice for long without sun, water, and you being able to tend to the plants.

Climbers and Vines

To make good use of vertical space, you can grow climbers and vines up walls, fencing, and trellises. Climbers and vines are a fantastic addition to any garden, and they can easily be grown in containers. You can use them as centerpieces or accents and backdrops for other plants. They can be trained up nearly any structure, and you can use them to draw attention to something like a wall or distract from an unsightly necessity like an air conditioning unit.[1]

Support is one of the most important things to consider when growing climbers and vines in containers. Support in pots can be as simple or as complex as you want it to be, and you can buy it or make it yourself. One of the easiest ways to make support is to stick small, straight branches into the soil around your plant, creating a structure the vines can climb. You can also spray paint bamboo poles and then use a zip tie or twine to fasten the poles together at the top. You can also attach a trellis to a wall and place vining plants in containers against it. If you're going for a more rustic look, you can set your container next to a fence or a support column and let nature take its course. If you choose to put your support in the pot itself, you should place it before the plant gets too big. You want the plant to be able to start climbing as soon as it can and don't want to disturb its root system.

There are lots of choices when it comes to climbers and vines, but my favorite are passion flower, morning glory, black-eyed Susan vine, cardinal climber, and moonflower. These are gorgeous flowering vines that can truly take your garden to the next level.

---

[1] Image from: https://balconygardenweb.com/container-vegetable-garden-design-ideas-tips/

Colorful Containers and Plants

This won't appeal to everyone, and some people may find bright colors too garish. Personally, I love bright colors, but you should go for what appeals to you, of course. You can inject a lot of color into your garden with brightly colored containers, flooring, trellises, and the plants you grow. You may opt for a color theme. I have a friend who loves their garden to be mostly a mix of purples and blues.

Edible Flowers

Growing edible flowers will give lovely color to your garden as well as make your dishes look beautiful and give them a fragrant floral flavor. Edible flowers include nasturtiums, pansies, lavender, roses, marigolds, calendula, and violets. You can use edible flowers in salads, and you can also make beautiful clear jellies with edible flowers set into them.

Exotic Plants

If you're feeling adventurous, you might want to try growing exotic plants and vegetables. You may wish to try growing black tomatoes, Mexican sour gherkin, Thai basil, dragon carrot,

_____

[2] Image from: https://plantersetcetera.com/blog/color-combinations-for-flower-pots/

Romanesco broccoli, or red perilla. This will be exciting to try growing and will give you something different to eat. And it will definitely be a talking point among any dinner guests, friends, or family.

Hanging Baskets

You can use hanging baskets to grow a wide variety of things, and they are a great way to diversify the look of your garden. It doesn't just have to be trailing plants. You can grow vegetables, such as tomatoes, or fruits, such as strawberries, in hanging baskets, and a nice selection of herbs too. Hanging baskets can be as simple as growing a single type of plant, or you can mix and match a variety of different plants or flowers for maximum impact.

Herbs

Growing herbs in your container garden is always a great idea. They smell fantastic and really enhance the garden. They will make your meals pop with flavor too. When we started using more herbs in our cooking, it really took our meals to a whole new level. You don't need to grow every herb that exists, but you could check out some recipes that appeal to you and first try to grow the herbs that would really accompany those dishes and get good use. It's lovely to always have fresh herbs at hand, and I personally think they are so much better than dried herbs.

You can opt for a one-pot herb garden. Below is an example of a one-pot herb garden and what this could look like.

ONE-POT HERB GARDEN HOW-TO

THYME

ROSEMARY

DILL

OREGANO

CHIVES

SAGE

Another suggestion is to have a 3-tier system. Essentially, this is 3 containers stacked on one another, with the largest pot at the bottom, then a medium pot, and then a small pot on top.

³ Image from: https://balconygardenweb.com/container-vegetable-garden-design-ideas-tips/

Large Plants at the Back, Small Plants at the Front

It can often be sensible to plant taller plants at the back of the garden, and shorter, lower growing plants at the front—this is done for practical reasons so that the taller plants don't block the light and don't obscure the view of the shorter ones.

Make a Focal Point

You can arrange and organize your container garden around a focal point, which will make it look magnificent and make it a pleasure to relax nearby. You may decide to plant a stunning looking shrub or a tree in a container that is eye catching, and this can be a focal point of your garden. Around the base of this, you could put more lower growing plants.

Movable Garden

I think this is a really sensible idea if your plants can't get the sunlight they require in the same spot continuously. While you can pick up some containers, it's a bit inconvenient to have to move lots of them. However, if you have a container that is on wheels, this will allow you to push it into the sunny places of your garden when required just as easily as pushing a shopping cart.

One-Pot Vegetable Garden

If you are really limited for space, you could have a one-pot vegetable garden, for example, on a balcony or a window box in which you can grow chives, basil, radishes, tomatoes, and so on.

Salad Table

A salad table is a great way to grow different lettuces and leafy greens, such as spinach or kale. A salad table is exactly what it sounds like—a portable table just deep enough to grow salad greens, herbs, and other shallow-rooted plants. Salad tables typically have a mesh bottom that allows water to drain.

---

[4] Image from: https://balconygardenweb.com/container-vegetable-garden-design-ideas-tips/

The benefits of a salad table are that you won't have to kneel down to plant or harvest, you're highly unlikely to get any weeds, and rabbits and squirrels won't disturb your plants as easily. A salad table is the perfect solution if you want to grow some leafy greens and herbs but don't have enough space for containers or don't want to put in a raised bed.

The table can get pretty heavy once it's filled with soil, so you'll need someone to help you move it, or you can attach casters to the legs to make it easier to move around. Place your table somewhere sunny, and keep an eye out for snails and slugs so that they don't eat your plants.

---

5 Image from: https://www.creativegreenliving.com/2016/06/how-to-make-lettuce-table-from-cast-off-vintage-desk.html

Stakes

If you don't have a lot of space, staking your plants up will help you get the most out of the space you have available. This works well for many vegetables, including tomatoes, eggplants, beans, peas, and more. It's best to place a stake when a plant is still young so that it can climb up the stake. You can put stakes in pots at the same time you are planting your plants.

You can buy stakes made of bamboo or vinyl-coated metal at most garden centers. I would suggest placing a stake near the edge of a container and not in the center. This will give plants more room to grow. Once you've placed the stake in the pot, you'll need to tie your plant to the stake about 2/3 of the way up the stem, but be careful not to tie it too tight. This can damage your plant as it grows because the tie can cut into the plant's stem. Use stretchy ties to prevent this, such as special plant ties or strips of nylon. You can also use plant clips—they're easier to use than garden ties. Taller plants may need several ties at different points along the stem.

---

[6] Image from: https://www.bunnysgarden.com/garden-stakes/

Theme Gardens

Theme gardens can be fun. For example, you can have a "salad garden" that contains colorful lettuce, dwarf tomatoes, chives, beets, and parsley. You could have a "pizza garden" that contains tomatoes, peppers, and basil. Or you could have a garden that has edible flowers, such as nasturtiums, marigolds, and pansies.

Trees in Containers

I'm a huge fan of growing trees in containers, and I think there's no better tree than a lemon tree. Lemons are absolutely perfect for sweet and savory dishes and different drinks. There are so many uses for lemons, even when it comes to household cleaning (mixed with bicarbonate of soda) or highlighting hair naturally. Lemons are a really lovely fruit that smells so fresh and vibrant and automatically gives you energy and a spring in your step. You can find more information on growing fruit trees in containers in Chapter 9.

Variety is the Spice of Life

It can be nice to vary the height of plants in a container garden, and you can easily do this by using plant stands or putting pots on upturned plant pots or buckets as a base for them. If a pot is large or heavy, then it's best to keep it on the ground for safety reasons so that it doesn't cause any damage to the pot, the plant or plants growing in it, people, or pets from being precariously balanced on something else.

You can use pedestal pots or pedestal stands that help show off plants and allow for plants to trail down. You can use brightly colored or patterned pots to inject some color into your garden. You can intersperse the pots with large stones, pebbles, water features, or ornaments.

Personally, I am a big fan of water features because I find it really relaxing to have the gentle trickle of water fountains as well as having the lovely smell of plants and their amazing colors. There is no right or wrong when it comes to designing your container garden. You can buy brightly colored or unusually shaped planters if they appeal to you. It's exactly like interior decorating—it's all about creating something that you find aesthetically pleasing to look at. This is all that matters!

Vertical Planters

Vertical planters look lovely and don't take up much room. They can take less room than a laundry drying rack. You could easily use a vertical planter to grow lettuce, fresh herbs, or leafy greens. You can be quite inventive regarding what you use for vertical planters. You can use things like bookshelves, plant holders, and shoe racks.

You may choose to put several plants in one large container rather than having each of them separately in small containers. This can look really clean and well-organized. Personally, I like a wide range of colors, patterns, shapes, and sizes in my own garden.

If there are things in your garden that you'd like to block from view, such as a shed, or if you want to add privacy and block your neighbors' view of your backyard, then using containers filled with conifers, bamboo, or grasses is a beautiful way to create a screen.

You may choose to have pots that contrast with the colors of the plants you put in them to really make the colors pop and stand out. You can use the spiller, filler, and thriller technique to ensure plants are combined beautifully.

I used to grow plants in my backyard during the summer months, and I loved the display I put together. Because they were in containers that were easily portable, I was able to move them inside the house during the colder months. This meant the plants were protected from the cold, and I didn't lose any plants over the winter. My front room has huge patio windows, so the plants received lots of natural sunlight throughout the day and were kept warm.

Key takeaways from this chapter:

1. When planning the location for your container garden, consider natural sunlight, water, and how accessible the containers are.

2. It's worth measuring what space you have available and keeping these measurements with you when you buy containers or plants.

3. Most vegetables require 6–8 hours of sunlight per day to grow well.

4. Leafy greens and herbs will grow in indirect sunlight.

5. Consider where you will get water for your plants from.

6. Ensure you have adequate access to tend to plants.

7. There is a wide variety of ways you can design your container garden, from using climbers/vines to colorful containers, edible flowers, exotic plants, salad tables, stakes, and hanging baskets. Always try to plant larger plants at the back and smaller plants at the front. Consider making a focal point in your garden. You could plant fruit trees in containers, such as apple, cherry, fig, peach, or citrus trees. You can add variety with

different shapes and colors of containers as well as different patterns and designs. You can add in features, such as rocks, pebbles, and water features. You can use vertical planters, and these make great use of space, working on a similar principle to skyscrapers.

The next chapter will look at creating the perfect growing medium. This is essential for your plants to grow well and thrive. So, the chapter will look at soil quality and what makes a good potting soil. It will also cover how you can mix different types of soil for optimum results and testing soil. Finally, it will cover how to make your own compost and how to use it in your container garden.

Chapter 4: Creating the Perfect Growing Medium

This chapter will look at creating the perfect growing medium for the plants in your container garden. You want the best growing medium for your plants that will help them thrive. Like with humans, if we don't get enough nutrients, we will be unhealthy and may suffer from deficiencies. It's exactly the same with plants and the soil you put them in.

There are different types of potting soil and potting mixes you can use in containers. Some soils are better than others, and there are specific soils for certain plants. This chapter will take you through soil quality and what makes a good potting soil in detail. It will also discuss how you can make your own potting soil. Finally, the chapter will end with how you can test soil for quality, with some suggestions for what you can do to improve it if it's not quite as good as you expected it to be.

When you're considering potting soil, one of the key choices will be whether you use a purely soilless growing medium or whether you decide to mix in some garden soil. This may come down to budget because using a purely soilless growing medium is more expensive, but it's sterile

---

[7] Image from: https://getbusygardening.com/potting-soil-for-container-gardening/

and less prone to pests and diseases. When you go to buy potting soil, you will find there's potting soil and potting mix available. Even though these terms are often used interchangeably, there is a difference between the two. Potting soil may contain soil. Potting mix is completely soilless and sterile, which makes it safer for plants because it doesn't contain pathogens such as fungus or other diseases.

Potting mixes are typically light and fluffy and have good aeration and drainage, while potting soil is heavy and dense and has worse aeration and drainage than potting mix. Potting mixes have worse longevity than potting soil, though. They contain peat moss and other organic matter that will eventually decompose, leading to soil compaction and nutrient depletion, and you would typically need to change the mix every 6 months and repot the plant. Potting soil will also degrade and become compacted over time, but you would typically need to change it only once a year. Another thing to consider is that potting mixes are more expensive than potting soil. But once you know what is needed to mix your own growing medium, this can help reduce costs. I personally prefer using potting mix in containers. I make my own potting mixes, and I will cover how you can make your own potting soil or potting mix later in this chapter.

It is important to have good soil in your containers because nutrients in potting soil don't regenerate like in garden soil, and the roots of the plants can't go beyond the container and explore further afield like they can in the ground to find the nutrients they need. Plants in containers are entirely dependent on the nutrients that you provide for them.

Fillers at the Bottom of Containers to Reduce Cost

It can cost a fair bit of money to fill containers with potting mix, especially if they are large and you have quite a number of them. What many people do, and it's a good idea, is place fillers at the bottom of containers.

You could crush aluminum cans, use plastic milk cartons, or some other non-biodegradable packaging. You can fill either a quarter or up to a third of a container with this material, then top it with landscape fabric. Then you can put your potting soil on top of it. The fabric acts as a barrier to stop the potting soil from mixing with your filler, but it allows the water to drain through, and there should still be sufficient space for your plants' roots.

Soil Quality

When you have good potting soil, it will help with drainage, water retention, and nutrient uptake by the plants. Good drainage for container plants is essential because otherwise too much moisture will accumulate near the roots of plants, and this could rot them and cause the plants to die.

Most potting mixes that you buy ready mixed contain peat, coir fiber, or vermiculite, and most don't have soil. Potting mixes are light and filled with air, even when they have been watered. Potting mix shouldn't become too compacted because this could suffocate roots and prevent a good flow of water and nutrients.

Read the label of the potting soil or potting mix you're intending to buy and see if it's made for a specific type of plant. Most outdoor plants will do well in all-purpose potting soil or potting mix for containers. If you are able to look inside the bag before you purchase it, you can ensure the soil has good consistency and doesn't contain lots of stones, grit, or pebbles.

Light and Fluffy

You can tell a high-quality potting mix because it will be light, fluffy, and will hold moisture. Potting soil can contain organic plant-based or animal-based materials, such as rice hulls, sphagnum moss, bark, manure, poultry litter, earthworm castings, coconut coir, peat moss, or coconut husks. Sometimes inorganic natural materials can be used too, and these will help the soil to retain moisture and have good drainage. These will include things like perlite, vermiculite, cinders, sand, and pumice.

Contains Fertilizer

Both potting soil and potting mix usually contain fertilizers that give nutrients to plants. Fertilizers can release after a certain amount of time, and it can be a blend of bone meal, kelp meal, and alfalfa meal. It is best to avoid chemical fertilizers if you're growing vegetables and fruits that you intend to eat. Potting soil may contain some other additives, such as lime to balance the pH, some beneficial microbes, and other things to help keep in moisture. If you buy commercial potting soil and it doesn't have the list of ingredients on the packaging, I'd suggest avoiding that.

With container plants, the nutrients are washed away each time you water, therefore you will need to fertilize the plants often to provide them with the nutrients they need to produce fresh, delicious vegetables and fruits for you. If your potting soil or potting mix doesn't have any fertilizer, you'll need to add some compost or a slow-release granular fertilizer at the time of planting. Then you will need to fertilize your plants with a liquid fertilizer every few weeks during the growing season. I'd suggest using organic fertilizers and avoiding chemical fertilizers—they can burn the roots of your plants, and you don't want to be eating food that has been grown with chemicals. I use organic fertilizers, such as bone meal, blood meal, fish meal, and seaweed. You can also make compost tea from compost and use it as a liquid fertilizer for your plants, which will be covered later in this chapter.

No Pebbles, Sand, or Bugs

If you see bugs crawling out of the bag or bugs hovering around the bag, I wouldn't purchase it. If you feel the bag, and it feels sandy or like there's lots of pebbles or large grit in it, again, I wouldn't buy this. The soil should have an earthy smell but shouldn't smell of anything else. It shouldn't smell unpleasant.

Never Just Use Garden Soil, Topsoil, or Compost for Containers

Do not use just garden soil in containers because it's often too compacted, which means it won't be able to drain effectively and your plants' roots may rot. Garden soil just doesn't offer enough air, water, or nutrients to container plants.

Topsoil is from the very top of gardens, and it can vary in quality, but it's usually less nutrient rich than other garden soil, so I would advise that you do not use this type of soil in containers because it can contain rocks, pebbles, and not many nutrients. You can sometimes buy topsoil in bags, which is sedge peat. This doesn't drain well and is poorly aerated. You could use this instead of garden soil when mixing your own potting soil, but it should never just be used on its own.

Garden soil can also contain trigs, spores, seeds, and diseases that could kill your plants. It's also never a good idea to solely use compost in your containers. It would be fine to add compost to potting soil or potting mix, vermiculite, or perlite, but just on its own it's not a good idea. Investing in good potting soil is a worthwhile investment because ultimately, you'll get an abundance of delicious vegetables and fruits that are full of vitamins and minerals.

Different Soils for Different Plants

There are different types of potting soils and potting mixes for different purposes. There is all-purpose potting soil or potting mix that you can use indoors and outdoors in different types of containers—this is a good all-rounder to grow different plants in, and this is what I would suggest to a beginner to container gardening. There are potting soils and potting mixes made specifically for indoor plants. There are potting soils and potting mixes for different types of plants, such as cacti, African violets, and orchids. And there is also seed starting mix specifically for starting seeds.

If you're growing herbs, perennials, and succulents, these need soil that drains well and does not retain a lot of moisture for long, and the growing medium can be coarse with bark, perlite, or sand. If you're growing tropical plants or plants that have a lot of foliage, they may want more peat in the soil and more moisture.

Commercial potting soil mixes can vary widely in pH levels. The pH scale ranges from 0 to 14. The lower end of the scale is acidic and the higher end is alkaline. The middle point—7.0— is neutral. Most plants prefer to grow in soil with a pH level between 6.0 and 7.5. Few plants, such as blueberries, need acidic soil with a pH level between 4 and 5.5. You can get potting mixes to match different plants' needs. As mentioned previously, most plants will grow well in an all-purpose potting mix, so you don't need to worry about it too much. Measuring and adjusting the pH level of your potting soil will be covered a bit later in the next section of this chapter.

New Potting Soil or Potting Mix Over Time

One thing that is worth noting regarding potting soil and potting mix is that the longer you have it, the more the nutrients in it decompose and become less useful to plants. Potting soil can also develop pathogens and could have spores or bugs from previous plants. You would typically need to replace potting mix every 6 months and potting soil every year. I would also recommend against reusing potting soil or potting mix. I would suggest having fresh soil each time you start growing new plants to give them the best start in life.

If you've opened a bag of potting soil, I'd suggest using it within half a year. If it's unopened, you can use it within a year. You can put used soil in a compost pile or add it to your raised beds or garden beds. If you've ever experienced a diseased plant, I would never ever use that potting soil again. If you have really large or very deep containers, you might not have to replace all the soil, but I would suggest replacing the top three quarters of it ideally.

Wet Perlite and Vermiculite and Wear a Mask

As a health and safety tip, it is a good idea to wear a face mask if you're using potting soil because it's not great to breathe in perlite or vermiculite as they're not healthy for your lungs. You could wet both perlite and vermiculite before using to stop the dust flying up in the air and being breathed in.

Mixing Potting Soil

If you decide to make your own potting soil or potting mix, it's good to do research on the types of plants you want to grow in containers to find out what their preferred soil conditions are. You can add garden soil to the mix because this will give some bulk to it and also some much-needed nutrients. But you do need to ensure that the soil is healthy and free from diseases or pests. Some people are completely against using any garden soil and would always advocate pure soilless potting mixes. Soil and compost mixes are heavier, which is fine for plant pots on the ground, especially the ones you want to prevent from blowing over. But it may be too heavy for hanging planters. It may sound an obvious point, but when the soil has been watered, it's much heavier too.

As general guidance (though do be sure to research your plants' specific needs) you can make a potting soil base mix with one part garden soil, one part peat moss, and one part perlite or coarse builders sand. You should never use sand from the beach or play sand.

There are advantages and disadvantages to mixing potting soil yourself. By using soil from the garden, it can contain good things like worms and nutrients. But it may also contain harmful insects, weed seeds, and disease organisms too. Because potting mixes that don't contain soil are sterile and free of these, it's a safer environment for plants to grow in.

Non-soil-based growing mediums are lighter. When you use soil, this will make a heavier soil mix. This could be beneficial if you live in a windy area and having a heavier pot would help prevent it from tipping over. Using garden soil as part of the mix means that the pot won't drain or dry out as quickly. Buying soilless mixes can be expensive, so by adding garden soil to your mix, it can mean that the growing medium lasts longer and can be used in more pots.

If you know you have a lot of containers to fill, you can buy large bags of potting soil ingredients in bulk and mix them together. You can make a great soilless potting mix that can be adjusted according to the needs of your plants by mixing the following ingredients:

- 1 part peat moss—this is very light and airy and isn't compacted like garden soil. It can be a little difficult to get it moist, so it's sensible to put water on this before you mix it with other ingredients.

- 1 part compost or worm castings (or a mix of these two)—this will give the soil wonderful nutrients. You could mix a few different types of compost to feed your plants better. We have used mushroom compost in the past and have had good results with it. You can also include leaf mold, which will offer nutrients.

- 1 part vermiculite or perlite—I like vermiculite better because it retains water, whereas perlite stops the soil from being compacted but doesn't retain water. Perlite and vermiculite are lightweight volcanic rocks that contain air. Perlite doesn't decompose with time, and it will always aerate. Vermiculite also contains potassium and magnesium, which are excellent nutrients for your plants.

- If you live in a particularly hot area, you may want to add a moisture hold product, such as little jelly crystals that absorb water from the soil and then release it gradually back in.

- Another great tip is to have extra mineral aggregate or organic materials at hand for plants that require these. If plants like their soil dry, you can add aggregate. If plants like moist soil, you can add peat moss. If plants are top-heavy, you can add calcined clay or sand to add weight to the pot and prevent it from tipping over.

Here's my favorite recipe for mixing potting soil. We've been using it for years and have always had great success with it:

- 2 gallons (7.6L) of peat moss
- 2 gallons (7.6L) of perlite
- 2 gallons (7.6L) of compost
- 2 gallons (7.6L) of garden soil
- ½ cup of dolomitic limestone
- ½ cup of soybean meal
- ½ cup of greensand
- ½ cup of rock phosphate
- ½ cup of kelp powder

Simply mix all the ingredients together and ensure everything is mixed. Then you can use it for all your container plants.

Here's another recipe devised by Cornell University. We've been using it for a while and have had great results with it.

- 1 bushel (8 gallons or 35.2 L) of peat moss
- 1 bushel (8 gallons or 35.2 L) of vermiculite
- ½ lb (227 g) of dolomitic limestone
- 1 lb (454 g) of 5-10-5 fertilizer
- 1.5 oz (42.5 g) of 20% superphosphate fertilizer

Again, this should all be mixed together. It's sensible to wet the mixture as you're stirring to make this easier. Keep in mind that superphosphate fertilizer in this mix is not organic. I adapted this recipe for organic gardening by substituting synthetic fertilizers with organic ones. We have been using this modified recipe for quite a while and it works really well. Here is the recipe:

- 1 bushel (8 gallons or 35.2 L) of peat moss
- 1 bushel (8 gallons or 35.2 L) of perlite or vermiculite
- 1 lb (454 g) bone meal
- ½ lb (227 g) ground limestone
- ½ lb (227 g) blood meal

Always make sure to measure the pH level of your potting soil or potting mix. You can purchase pH testing kits online or at your local garden center. The instructions are easy to follow, and you will likely have to mix a sample with water and other ingredients and put in a test strip. If the level is outside of the range, you may need to adjust or change the soil.

You can use sulfur or aluminum sulfate to lower soil pH level (make it more acidic). You can also use peat moss or fresh pine needles to lower your soil pH level, but these are usually not as effective and don't work as quickly as sulfur or aluminum sulfate. To increase soil pH level (make soil less acidic), you can add finely ground agricultural limestone. The amounts of sulfur, aluminum sulfate, or lime should be carefully measured before adding, so check with your local garden center.

If you can master making your own potting soil and potting mixes, you will be able to fill up your containers with high-quality growing medium much more cheaply than buying commercial potting soil.

If you are reusing any containers that have been used for growing previously, it's really important to wash them thoroughly. Get any old soil out of them and use some dish soap and a small amount of bleach to thoroughly clean and sanitize them. Make sure to rinse them thoroughly after cleaning and leave them to air dry.

When you fill your containers, it's sensible to leave at least an inch of space at the top so that the soil isn't going to just flow over the edge of the pot when you water your plants.

Testing Soil

Testing soil will take a little patience. I know that once you have your containers, potting soil, and plants, it's all too tempting to just get straight to planting things up immediately. But it can be worthwhile testing your soil before putting your plants in it.

1. To test soil, get a medium-sized pot and fill it with potting soil directly from the bag.

2. Next, water the soil thoroughly with your watering can and watch how long it takes for the water to pass through the soil and come out of the drainage hole.

3. Leave this pot containing the wet soil for a couple of days in the place where you plan to have your container garden.

4. Return to the container after a few days and place your fingers into the soil. Is the soil soggy? Has it dried out completely? Is it like a mud pie? Or is it dry and crumbly?

Ideally, it should be neither soggy nor too dry. If soil is soggy, this may damage and rot the roots of your plants. You can add buiders sand or vermiculite until the soil is fluffier.

If the soil dries out too quickly, you want some moisture to be retained so that you don't have to water it many times a day when it's hot. To help with this, you could add some coco coir or compost, again, until it is fluffy.

There is also another way to test your soil. Get a plant pot and fill it with soil. Water it as you would normally do. Then, instead of walking away, water it again. If water stays on top of the soil, then the drainage in the mix is not adequate. You can resolve this by mixing in pumice, perlite, or bark to help with the drainage.[8]

---

[8] Image from: https://www.treehugger.com/test-your-potting-soil-quality-soil-planting-your-container-garden-4857230

How to Make Compost and Use It

Compost is decayed organic material that has decomposed into a state that it can be used as fertilizer for growing plants. Three key things needed to produce compost are nitrogen, carbon, and water. Compost is often given the name "black gold" because it is so valuable to the health of your soil and plants. It is also versatile, as it has multiple uses in the garden. You can add compost to potting soil or potting mix at the time of planting, or you can use it as mulch, which is essentially a covering for the soil that helps keep in moisture, keep the soil and plants' roots cool, and also helps reduce weeds. You can also make compost tea, which is a liquid fertilizer that you can use to feed your plants throughout the growing season.

Garden centers sell compost in bags, and you can buy it if that's more convenient for you. But it's easy enough to make compost yourself from leaves and grass trimmings from your garden, any paper or cardboard from your house, and things like food scraps, vegetables that haven't been used, eggshells, tea bags, coffee grounds, fruit scraps, and so on.

You can purchase a compost bin or build a compost pile. This choice will depend on how much space you have and how much compost you need. If you have a small garden and not a lot of space, you should get a compost bin. There are even small bins that you can keep in your kitchen. Modern composters are streamlined and odor-free. There are many styles of compost bins to choose from. They come in different sizes and can even fit into small apartments. Or you can get larger outdoor versions, which are essentially a barrel with a crank that makes it easy to keep the contents mixed. If you need a lot of compost and have some free space in your garden, you can build a compost pile with wooden pallets or spare wood where you can store nitrogen items and carbon items separately and then an area where these are layered together.

To make compost, you need to mix "green" materials (nitrogen), "brown" materials (carbon), and moisture. Green materials include kitchen scraps, such as vegetable or fruit peel, fruits or vegetables that haven't been used, eggshells, plants, coffee grounds, and grass trimmings. Brown materials include fallen leaves, tree branches, cardboard, newspapers, hay, straw, and wood shavings. You should have equal parts of green and brown materials. I would suggest alternating layers of green and brown materials. The final ingredient is moisture. Simply spray water on the compost pile to moisten it, but don't make it soggy. If it's too wet, it won't decompose properly.

There are things which you shouldn't put in a compost bin or pile, and this is because they will rot and smell bad and may attract rodents or larger wildlife. Do not add the following to your compost pile: meat or fish, dairy, fats and oils, any preserved wood, any diseased plants or invasive weeds (as these could be passed onto your plants via the compost and keep spreading and growing). Don't put charcoal ash into the compost pile because this could kill good bacteria, and definitely don't add dog or cat waste because it could contain harmful bacteria or parasites, and you don't want that in the soil that your plants are growing in.

The compost pile should heat up in order to decompose at a good rate. You can start your compost pile at any point throughout the year, but it will decompose quicker in the summer than in the winter.

To keep the decomposition rate on track, you'll need to take the temperature of your compost pile using a compost thermometer deep enough to get about 2/3 of the way down. You can buy these online or at some garden centers. Make sure to take the temperature in several spots. The ideal temperature is between 130 and 140°F (55–60°C). If it gets up to 160°F (71°C) or more, you need to turn the pile with a pitchfork to aerate it, which will help bring the temperature down. If the temperature gets to 170°F (76°C) or above for more than several hours, this will stop microbes from working and kill the decomposing process. Try to keep the average temperature of your compost pile around 135°F (57°C).

If the compost starts to smell unpleasant, it could be that you have too much nitrogen (green material), and you need to balance it with some brown materials. A properly balanced compost pile should not have any unpleasant smells, in fact, it should have a pleasant, earthy smell. If your pile starts to dry out, water it. You should it keep it moist but not soggy. You would typically need to water your compost pile once or twice a week. You should turn the pile every 2–4 weeks with a pitchfork. Once the pile starts to cool down and look like a black, crumbly material, then your compost is ready to use in the garden.

You can add compost to your potting soil or potting mix at the time of planting. You can mix 25% to 50% compost with potting soil or potting mix. When you add compost to your potting soil or potting mix, it can reduce the need for fertilizers. You can also use it as mulch. It will help keep your soil and plants' roots cool and retain moisture. You can also mulch containers to help some plants get through frosty weather. This will keep the roots warm and will prevent the roots of tender plants from being damaged. You can also make compost tea from compost, which is a liquid organic fertilizer. Fertilizing your plants, mulching your containers, and making compost tea will be covered in more detail in Chapter 6.

My preference for soil for starting out to grow plants in is to mix potting soil with some compost, peat moss, vermiculite, and moisture hold crystals. This mix has great drainage and water retention and contains a lot of nutrients to help your plants thrive.

Key takeaways from this chapter:

1. Potting soil and potting mix are not the same thing. Potting soil may have soil. Potting mix is soilless.

2. Decide between a soilless growing medium or a mix with some garden soil.

3. Leave an inch at the top of containers, so when you water them, the soil and water don't flow over the edge.

4. Place filler at the bottom of large containers to reduce costs.

5. Good quality potting soil should be light, fluffy, and hold moisture well. It should contain vermiculite or perlite and organic fertilizer. It should have no pebbles, sand, and no smell.

6. Never use just garden soil or topsoil in your containers because they are often too compacted, lack nutrients, may have pests, diseases, and weed seeds, and your plants won't grow well in them. Also, don't use just compost in your containers. It would be fine to add compost to potting soil or potting mix, vermiculite, or perlite, but just on its own it's not a good idea.

7. Ensure the soil you have meets the needs of your plants.

8. Don't reuse potting soil—put it in your compost instead. It loses nutrients over time and could contain pests and diseases from previous plants.

9. If you're mixing perlite or vermiculite, it's best to wet it and wear a face mask for safety.

10. You can create your own potting soil or potting mix by buying ingredients in bulk and mixing them together.

11. If you're reusing containers, ensure they are thoroughly cleaned and sanitized.

12. Making compost is not difficult—all you need is a compost bin, green materials (nitrogen), brown materials (carbon), and water. You'll need to water and turn your compost pile regularly. Once it's ready, you can use compost as fertilizer by mixing it with the potting soil at the time of planting, or you can use it as mulch. You can also make compost tea, which is an organic liquid fertilizer for your plants.

13. You can test soil by watering it and seeing the results after a few days or by watering it again right away to see how well it drains.

The next chapter will delve into the exciting topic of starting your container garden, looking carefully at the differences between seeds and seedlings and the pros and cons of starting a garden with each. The chapter will look at how you can start seeds and how to plant seedlings. It will also cover propagating plants from cuttings.

Chapter 5: Starting Your Container Garden

This chapter will cover everything you need to know about starting your container garden. Now you know that you want to start a garden and the various benefits and drawbacks of doing so and have the tools and containers you require. You know where best to position these in your garden or the space you have available and have selected the growing medium to help your plants thrive. The very next step is one of the most exciting—deciding whether you will grow your plants from seed or seedlings.

Seeds and Seedlings

When you're purchasing plants, you may have to compromise a little depending on what sunlight and space you have available. For example, you may want to grow tomatoes, but if where you live does not get lots of sunlight, then this isn't practical. You may want cucumbers, but if you don't have space for the vine to grow, you may have to pick other vegetables instead.

If the space where you will place the containers gets 6–8 hours of direct sunlight, you can pick sun-loving plants. If you have indirect sunlight, then you could grow leafy greens, herbs, and some shade-loving plants. If you live somewhere that is completely in the shade, you could grow some medicinal plants and houseplants that need little sunlight, for example, the snake plant, properly known as sansevieria.

The difference between seeds and seedlings is that with seeds, you plant them, and new plants will grow from these. Seedlings are young plants that have already sprouted and have grown. You would usually start seeds indoors. Seedlings can start off indoors until they're a bit hardier, and then they can be planted outside. You can start off seeds by putting them in a moist paper towel or growing them in a seed starting tray. You can buy packets of seeds from garden centers or online.

If you're trying to decide whether you should be buying seeds or seedlings, here are some things you may want to think about. Are the plants you want to grow easy to germinate from seed? Is the growing season long enough for the plants to mature if they are grown from seed? Will they require special care to grow well from seed? Will they transplant well? Always read seed packets thoroughly because they will give you a wealth of information and make it easier to make an informed decision about them. The seed packet tells you how long it takes for the plant to reach maturity. You won't get produce from the plant until it has reached maturity, so if this says 60 days, you won't get any vegetables or fruits until after this time. The packet will also give you a good indication about what time of year you should be sowing seeds.

9

The pros and cons of starting your plants from seed and buying seedlings will be covered below:

Pros and Cons of Starting Your Plants from Seed

Pros

- Seeds are inexpensive. By spending a small amount of money, you can grow lots of different plants.

- Some crops, such as beans, are quick to germinate, and it can be a good thing to start these from seed.

- When you choose seeds, you have a wide variety available that you can choose from, whereas with seedlings you only really have a choice of what is provided.

- If you start your plants from seed, it allows you to start gardening before spring officially starts by getting the seeds started indoors and ready to plant when it's warm enough, usually after the last frost.

---

[10] Image from: https://www.thespruce.com/vegetable-garden-seeds-or-seedlings-1403412

Cons

- Seeds take longer to grow than seedlings because seedlings have already started the growing stage and are bigger and stronger.

- It may not be practical for long-season plants in places with short growing seasons, so plants like tomatoes, peppers, or eggplants are often bought as potted plants from a nursery.

- Seeds typically need to be started indoors initially until they're hardy enough to be planted outside.

- When you start your plants from seed, there is a higher chance of things going wrong, such as adverse weather conditions, pests, and weeds.

Pros and Cons of Buying Seedlings

Pros

- Because seedlings are already more mature than seeds, you'll get your harvest quicker than when growing from seed.

- Seedlings can usually be grown outside, but you may need to bring them inside at night if they're young or fragile.

- Seedlings are more resistant to pests because they're more mature and stronger.

Cons

- Buying seedlings is more expensive than growing from seed.

- There's often not as much choice or variety—you just have what the nursery has available. There are a lot more plant varieties available via seeds.

- By introducing seedlings into your container garden, you run the risk that you could bring weeds or diseases that could harm your other plants. Therefore, if you're buying seedlings, it is important to get them from a reputable supplier to prevent this.

Other Considerations

- They don't like to be covered because they can get too moist, and then this attracts fungi and aphids. Seedlings like fresh air.

- Some seedlings like to start out indoors, and then be transplanted to containers outside. The types of vegetables that do this include artichoke, basil, broccoli, Brussels sprouts, cabbage, cauliflower, celery, chard, chives, collard greens, eggplant, kale, leeks, mustard, parsley, peppers, and tomatoes.

Roots or Bulbs

Some vegetables are grown from root divisions or bulbs. This can include asparagus, garlic, horseradish, onions, potatoes, rhubarb, and sweet potatoes.

Other Considerations

Some plants can be started from seed indoors and then be transplanted into containers outside. Plants that can be started indoors and then transplanted include artichoke, basil, broccoli, Brussels sprouts, cabbage, cauliflower, celery, chard, chives, collard greens, eggplant, kale, leeks, mustard, parsley, peppers, and tomatoes.

Some plants don't transplant well and should be planted directly in the containers that you plan to grow them in. Plants that should be started directly in containers include beans, beets, carrots, corn, garlic, okra, parsnips, pumpkins, radishes, squash, turnips, watermelons, and zucchini.

Starting Seeds

If you want to start gardening early in the season, growing your plants from seed is a great way to start. You need fresh seeds that have been stored correctly to grow well. Ensure that you buy your seeds from a reputable company. I strongly suggest getting organic seeds. Organic seeds are seeds taken from plants grown without the use of synthetic fertilizers and pesticides, which means they are better for you and for the environment. Plants grown from organic seeds are also naturally better at fending off pests on their own.

Check the seed packet to see if the plants you want to grow would grow well in your location. You could look for regionally based companies with seeds that thrive in your area. Regional suppliers are less likely to offer seeds that are unsuited to your growing conditions.

When you are choosing vegetables to plant, do look on the back of packets or in the seed catalog for seeds that have characteristics of being disease resistant because this will give you better quality vegetables and may reduce pests that come into your garden. While you can keep seeds for a few years, it is preferable to buy new seeds each year to ensure you get a better crop.

Also, check the seed packet or information for details about what conditions they like to grow in and the best time to sow them. Most seed packets will tell you if they can be started indoors and then transplanted or sown directly in containers. They will usually tell you how long it will take for the plants to produce edible produce (days to maturity), and they should tell you their light and water requirements. Some may give information about the type of soil the plant likes.

Make a list of the vegetables and herbs that you enjoy eating, and then think about where these would grow in your garden space. If you're a complete beginner to container gardening, I would suggest starting out with easy-to-grow vegetables rather than ones that are known to be difficult so that it doesn't spoil your fun by being complicated. Lettuce, green beans, peas, radishes, carrots, cucumbers, kale, Swiss chard, beets, and zucchini are all relatively easy to grow. Tomatoes and peppers require a bit more care, but they are not terribly difficult to grow. Cauliflowers, eggplants, celery, and watermelons can be more difficult to grow.

If you don't like certain vegetables, don't grow them because if you don't enjoy eating them, it'll probably be just wasted time and food, unless you plan to sell them. Remember that if you're growing peas, pole beans, cucumbers, tomatoes, or other vining plants, you'll need to have trellises to support them when they grow, and also remember that they may create shade as they grow, so take this into consideration.

You can also do wonders by harvesting seeds from existing fruits to grow in the future. You can do this with cucumbers, peppers, tomatoes, strawberries, and many others. This will be covered in more detail a bit later.

You can start seeds indoors—usually before the last frost—so that your seedlings are ready to be transplanted outside to the garden when the weather is warmer. Seed packets may say things like: "Plant inside 6 to 8 weeks before the last frost". You would typically start seeds in a seed starting tray or in small containers and then transplant the seedlings into bigger containers when they grow too big before finally transplanting them into your growing containers.

You can start seeds in seed starting trays like below:

Or you can repurpose household plastic food packaging, from yoghurt pots to plastic bottles and trays that you get grapes, salad, or donuts in. If you're repurposing trays, make sure to poke holes in the bottom of the tray so that seeds have drainage. You can also use egg trays. You can even grow seeds on a moist kitchen towel.

Once you've chosen a container, you'll need to fill it with some seed starting mix. You can start seeds in potting mix, but most seeds, especially smaller ones, do better when started in seed starting mix, and it should be a fresh sterile mix. I would advise against starting seeds in potting soil and especially in garden soil because this can lead to fungal diseases and kill your seeds. Seed starting mix is a special form of soilless potting mix that typically uses smaller particles of vermiculite and sand, and it omits the organic materials found in standard potting soil. You can

---

[11] Image from: https://www.bhg.com/gardening/yard/garden-care/seed-starting-essentials/

loosen and dampen the seed starting mix before planting seeds, but don't soak it. If you start seeds in seed starting mix, you'll generally need to transplant the seedlings into a standard potting mix or potting soil when they begin to develop into larger plants.

You can make your own seed starting mix by mixing equal parts of coco coir, perlite, and vermiculite. Simply combine all the ingredients in a clean tub or bucket and water the mixture well. Stir the mixture with your hands or a trowel until it's moist but not soggy (like a wrung-out sponge). You can fill your seed starting trays or pots with this mix and sow seeds right away.

You can also make your own potting mix for transplanting your seedlings into when they grow. You can make a basic potting mix or an enriched one with compost. To make a basic potting mix, mix 6 parts coco coir, 1 part perlite, and 1 part vermiculite. Enriched potting mix is made by mixing 4 parts coco coir, 2 parts compost, 1 part perlite, and 1 part vermiculite. Simply combine all the ingredients in a clean tub or bucket, and water the mixture well, the stir it until it's moist, but not soggy.

You will need to moisten the growing medium so that it is wet throughout but not soaked. Look at the back of the seed packet. This should tell you how deep the seeds need to be planted. Some seeds need to be placed in holes, while other seeds may need to be sprinkled onto the growing medium (this is called surface sowing). If you don't have a packet, then a rule of thumb is to plant seeds to a depth that is twice their width.[12]

---

[12] Image from: https://www.bhg.com/gardening/yard/garden-care/seed-starting-essentials/

If you don't have a dibber (a tool for making holes to plant seeds into), you can simply use an old pencil to make a hole, drop the seed in, and then cover it with seed starting mix. It's a good idea to plant 2–3 seeds per hole because not every seed you plant will germinate. There isn't anything you're doing wrong, it's just nature. It's a really sensible idea to label the container with the name of what you have planted in it and the date you planted the seeds so that you can keep track of them.

If more than one seed grows, you can thin them out. It simply means you should let the strongest looking one grow, and cut the rest at the base. You should thin out seedlings when they have developed 1–2 true leaves. The very first leaves that grow from seed are called seed leaves or cotyledons. They are long and narrow in some plants, but in others they are heart shaped. True leaves come after seed leaves. They have the same shape as the adult foliage, just baby sized.

You will need to keep the seed starting mix moist but not soggy. You would typically need to water your seeds daily, and you can spray your seed starting mix with a spray bottle. You could also place a fan near them to improve air circulation.

You can cover your seeds with a clear plastic dome or wrap, and this will help them to germinate more quickly. You can purchase heating mats to germinate seeds because most seeds germinate well in temperatures between 65 and 75°F (18–24°C). Your seeds will need to be watered more if you use a heating mat.

Once the seedlings emerge, remove the plastic dome or wrap you had covering them. When the seedlings have started to grow, keep watering them the same way. Keep the soil or seed starting mix moist but not soggy—it should feel like a damp sponge. You would typically need to water your seedlings daily.

The packet your seeds came in will also give you information on how long they'll take to germinate. Seed packets may give advice such as "plant inside 6–8 weeks before the last frost". The last frost refers to the average final spring frost in your area. Last frost dates are only an estimate based on historical climate data and are not set in stone. In the US, the National Weather Service tracks this data and has created charts that show the average last frost dates for various areas. You can find them by simply going online and typing in the phrase "last frost date by zip", and you'll find websites where you can find the last frost date for your specific zip code.[13]

Seedlings do require a lot of light. If they're too far away from light once they've germinated, they'll start to get long and leggy because they reach for the light, but this will make them weaker. The only way to prevent seedlings from becoming leggy is to provide more light. You could use grow lights to give them more light. You can grow seedlings without grow lights on a

windowsill, but having grow lights will dramatically improve germination rate, and your seedlings will be much stronger and healthier.

Having adequate lighting is essential for growing seedlings successfully. When I was just starting out with gardening decades ago, I tried starting plants from seed indoors without artificial lighting. I was lucky to have a massive south-facing window in my living room, and that's where

---

[13] Image from: https://dearshari.com/tag/poppy/

I first tried starting seeds. That worked okay, but my seedlings were thin and leggy, especially compared to the ones you'd find in a garden center. Also, at least half of the seeds didn't sprout at all. And things got only worse when I tried starting different plants from seed. It was clear that they didn't get enough light from my large windowsill. That's when I decided to splurge on grow lights, and I was amazed at the difference it made! Almost all of my seeds started sprouting, the seedlings became much stronger and healthier, and they had no problem surviving the transition to my containers, raised beds, in-ground garden, and even hydroponic systems.

Clearly, to grow strong and healthy seedlings, you need to provide proper lighting for them right from the start. Having grow lights for seedlings has lots of benefits that will be covered below:

- More seeds will sprout: If you have grow lights, more seeds will sprout, so you can save some money by not having to plant extras to make up for some seeds not sprouting or growing weak.

- Stronger and healthier seedlings: Your seedlings will be much stronger and healthier and will have an easier time surviving the transition to containers.

- Proper lighting helps prevent legginess: When seedlings don't get enough light, they will try to reach for the sun and will become leggy. While they may look taller, they become thin and weak because of that. Having grow lights for seedlings is the only way to prevent legginess.

- Grow seeds in a convenient place: If you have grow lights, you can start seeds in a place that's convenient for you, so you won't be limited to a windowsill.

- Grow seedlings easier: Having grow lights will make your life much easier. You can put your grow lights on a timer, so you won't have to worry about whether your seedlings are getting enough light.

You would typically use fluorescent or LED (light-emitting diode) grow lights for starting seeds. Metal halide (MH) and high-pressure sodium (HPS) lights produce lots of heat and can burn seedlings. Fluorescent grow lights are cheaper than LEDs; however, LED grow lights have a few benefits over fluorescent grow lights.

LED grow lights are more energy efficient and produce more lumens per watt, so a compact LED grow light can produce more light than a bulky fluorescent light. They also have longer lifespan than other types of grow lights and don't lose effectiveness over time. Full-spectrum or RGB LED grow lights are more versatile because they can produce any color of light, so you can use them to grow plants from seed to harvest. Fluorescent lights are good for starting seeds and growing lettuce, salad greens, and flowers.

Seedlings need cool blue/white light to grow. Having full-spectrum grow lights is ideal for growing seedlings indoors because they can produce light that mimics natural sunlight. Fluorescent lights produce cool blue/white light, and they work well for starting seeds too.

LED grow lights can get quite expensive, so if you're not growing indoors and just want to get grow lights for starting seeds, then fluorescent grow lights will be fine. If you want to grow indoors, or if you're moving your plants indoors for the winter and you're not sure whether they'll get enough light, then you may consider getting LED grow lights. Even though the initial expense can be quite high, they will save you money over the long term because they are very energy efficient and versatile.

If you get grow lights for seedlings, you shouldn't leave the lights on all day long. Seedlings need 14–16 hours of light per day, so you should have your lights on a timer for convenience. Some people grow seedlings with 12 hours of light daily, but it's usually not enough in my experience. You can try that, but you should monitor your seedlings closely in this case. If they start getting tall and growing sideways, you should add 2 more hours of light per day.

How high you should have your grow lights above your seedlings depends on the type of lights you have. I'd suggest following the height recommendations provided by the light manufacturer. However, if that information isn't provided, fluorescent grow lights should be kept 2–3 inches (5–7.5 cm) above seedlings, and LED grow lights should be at least a foot (30 cm) above. You'll need to move your grow lights away from the seedlings as they grow.

I mentioned earlier that you can grow plants from existing fruits and vegetables. The fruits and vegetables you purchase from a shop contain seeds, for example, apple pips (in the core), strawberry seeds (on the outside), banana seeds inside bananas, cucumber seeds inside cucumbers, avocado stones, and so on. What I would strongly suggest, mostly just for fun, is to have a go at growing some plants from the seeds of existing fruits and vegetables. It doesn't cost much to give it a go, so you can scoop out some tomato seeds, or scrape off some strawberry seeds, or use a spoon to scoop out some seeds from a cucumber or a banana and plant these up, label them, and see what grows. You can grow peppers from the seeds inside them. You can wait for potatoes to grow tubers and try growing them. Go against the advice you were given as a child to "not play with your food" and give it all a go. There's nothing to lose and lots of fun and enjoyment to be had.

Issues with Seeds

If not all your seeds germinate, it's worth having another read of the back of the seed packet to see if you did everything it suggested in terms of temperature, light, and water. Have the seeds rotted because the soil was too moist? Or was the soil too dry, and the seeds dried out? Try again and try to follow the instructions and be consistent with how moist your soil is.

If your seedlings are tall, leggy, and spindly, it could be that they aren't getting enough light, so they're growing to try to reach the light. They should get 14–16 hours of bright light per day, which you can help along with grow lights. If the temperature is too warm, this can cause plants to be leggy too. If that's the case, you could reduce the temperature in the room and also use a little less fertilizer.

In the image on the next page, it shows the difference between the seeds on the left, which were grown under grow lights, and the seeds on the right, which were grown on a windowsill and have become leggy.

If your seedlings looked good, and then suddenly they toppled at the base, this could be due to a soilborne fungus known as damping off. Damping off can affect most seedlings, particularly under conditions of high humidity, poor air circulation, and if seeds were sown too thickly. It is mainly a problem when sowing early indoors.

If you have it in the soil, I would recommend getting rid of the soil and using a soilless growing medium instead because you can't get rid of it once it's there. This is why I recommend using seed starting mix, which is a soilless growing medium, for starting seeds in the first place. When I first tried to grow cucamelon seeds, I had this happen, and it was so frustrating to see little seeds starting to sprout and then just die for what seemed like no good reason. I then started using a seed starting mix to start seeds and never had this problem again.

If you have mold growing on the surface of the seed starting mix or potting mix, this is a sign that the growing medium is too wet. It may not harm the plants too much, but definitely stop watering them for a few days, and you could put a fan nearby too, which will help with air circulation. You can scrape off the mold or put the seedlings in fresh potting mix, but be really careful and try not to damage them.

---

[14] Image from: https://www.gardeners.com/how-to/how-to-start-seeds/5062.html

Growing and Potting Up Seedlings

If you have grown plants from seed yourself, and they have grown into thriving seedlings, you will likely have to pot these into larger pots at least once, if not more than once, before needing to move them out into your container garden.

They do need to be kept moist, but not soggy, so regularly mist them with a spray bottle. The best indicator that your seeds or seedlings need water is how dry their growing medium is. When you touch the potting mix, it should feel neither soggy nor too dry. Instead, it should feel like a moist sponge. When watering your seedlings, use a mister or a very gentle spray bottle to water the top of your seed tray or container.

If you have grow lights, remember to raise them as the seedlings grow so that you don't burn them. You could also have a fan in the room to keep air circulating well. You should fertilize seedlings when they grow to 3 inches (7.5 cm) with an organic liquid fertilizer and then weekly after that.

Once seedlings have grown to approximately 2 inches (5 cm) tall and have at least 3–4 true leaves, then they can be transplanted into larger containers outside with regular potting soil or potting mix rather than seed starting mix. The very first leaves on the seed are called seed leaves or cotyledons. They are long and narrow in some plants, but in others they are heart shaped. True leaves come after seed leaves. They have the same shape as the adult foliage, just baby sized.

However, if the weather is still too cold, you can continue growing seedlings indoors. You will have to pot them up as they grow, though. Potting up seedlings, whether you've grown them yourself or have purchased them from a nursery, just means putting them into larger containers so that they can grow, thrive, and produce wonderful vegetables, fruits, and herbs for you to enjoy eating. Seedlings need to be put into larger containers so that they have room for their roots to grow and don't become root bound.

If you haven't seen a root-bound plant before, the picture on the next page shows what one looks like. This is a tomato seedling that has been in a small container much too long. You can see how the roots have just grown into the container shape because they had nowhere else to go.

You can sometimes gently massage a root-bound plant before you transplant it into a bigger pot, but you need to be careful not to break the roots when you do this.

When you pot up seedlings, their roots will become bigger and will take up more water. Seedlings are always very thirsty and need lots of water to thrive. When you've put seedlings into their new containers, do remember to feed them because they'll want to take in as many good nutrients as they can to grow strong.

You can plant seedlings when plants are starting to look cramped and overgrown in their small seed starting trays. If plants have started out in 4-inch (10 cm) pots, then around 6–8 weeks after germination they can be moved into 6–8-inch (15–20 cm) pots.

The time for planting seedlings into bigger pots can depend on the plant too. Tomatoes will outgrow their pots very quickly, but herbs can take a bit more time. Tomatoes grow faster

---

[15] Image from: https://homesteadandchill.com/potting-up-seedlings/

than peppers, for example, so they will need to be planted sooner than peppers. Vegetables like squash grow fast and like a lot of room, so it can be fine to start squash in 6-inch (15 cm) pots.[16]

If your seedlings are starting to have their roots poke out of drainage holes, this is a key sign that they need to be transplanted into larger containers. You can pot up seedlings before this happens, but this is just a sign they're definitely ready to be put into larger containers.

One helpful tip when you're potting up seedlings is to make a "dummy hole" or placeholder with the existing container in the new container that the seedling is being transplanted into. You can fill the new container with potting soil, then place the existing container in it and

check that things are at the right level. Ensure the soil in the new container is moist. When you do this, it will help make sure that there are no air pockets around the plant, and it saves you having to tip in extra soil, which can get all over the leaves of the plant and be a bit awkward. It also means that transplanting of the seedling goes smoothly and stops the plant from being jostled about. Prior to learning about this tip, we often had over or underfilled containers and had to mess about with soil levels.

After you put your seedlings into new containers, you need to water them. Watering from below can work

[16] Image from: https://homesteadandchill.com/potting-up-seedlings/

nicely, and you could give them some diluted seaweed extract to help them along. Another thing seedlings like is aloe vera soil drench. This seems to prevent seedlings suffering from the shock of being transplanted and helps them develop strong roots.

When it comes to transplanting seedlings into containers outside, don't put them directly outside—the transition to being outside needs to be gradual. You can start by putting them in a protected place outdoors for a few hours, but bring them back inside at night because it might be too cold for them. Over 10 days, gradually let them get used to being outside more and more. After that, you can leave the containers outside. A cold frame is also a good place to harden off seedlings.

Propagating Plants from Cuttings

If you're just starting out with container gardening, you'll likely have to start plants from seed or purchase seedlings from a nursery. There is another way to start plants, however—from cuttings. It's exactly what it sounds like—you can use cuttings from existing plants to grow new plants. Taking cuttings from plants is a great way to propagate them. It is also called cloning. Some plants can be difficult to start from seed, so you can purchase a plant from a nursery and then propagate it via cuttings.

I have always adored taking plant cuttings. I love the fact that from one plant you can create numerous others and watch them grow. I do this with all my house plants, and I have done this with plants that I grow in containers too.

When you propagate plants this way, often the plant has done a lot of the growing work, and the new plants grow much quicker than from seed. Only take cuttings from healthy, strong plants. Take a few more cuttings than required because sometimes not all of the cuttings survive.

Here's what you'll need to propagate plants from cuttings:

- Existing plant (parent plant)
- Razor blade or scissors
- Pencil or stick
- Rooting hormone

- 2 small plastic cups
- Paper towels
- Soilless potting mix
- Clear plastic cover for seed starting tray or a plastic bag
- 4–6-inch (10–15 cm) containers or a seed starting tray
- Rubbing alcohol

You'll need a porous, soilless growing medium. You can make your own by mixing equal parts of sand, perlite, peat moss, and vermiculite. Do not add fertilizers or manure to this because they can burn cuttings.

You can start cuttings in seed starting trays, but larger plants may need a 4–6-inch (10–15 cm) deep container. You can also use are Styrofoam coffee cups or large paper cups, but make sure to poke a drainage hole at the bottom.

Here's how you propagate plants from cuttings:

1. Choose a healthy parent plant to take cuttings from. Don't take cuttings from diseased or wilting plants. The parent plant should have good, green growth and be large enough to take cuttings from.

2. Next, fill your seed starting tray or container with the growing medium and poke a hole in it with the pencil.

3. Now you'll need to find suitable stems for cutting. They should be green and non-woody. Newer growth is easier to root than older or woody stems. Find a stem with a node—a bump along the stem where a leaf or a flower bud attaches. New roots will emerge from it.

4. Sterilize your razor blade or scissors with rubbing alcohol and make a clean cut just below the node. The cutting doesn't need to be long, 4–6 inches (10–15 cm) is enough, but it should have at least 2 leaves and 1 node.

5. Once you've taken the cutting, you need to make a partial slice through the middle of the node with a sterilized razor blade. This will increase the chances of roots emerging

from this spot. If your cutting has more than 1 or 2 leaves—cut them off. The cutting only needs 1–2 leaves to continue photosynthesis. Having too many leaves will consume energy that would otherwise go to root creation. If the leaves are very large in relation to the stem, you can cut off the top halves of the leaves too.

6. Next, you'll need to dip the cutting in the rooting hormone. Rooting hormones are typically not organic; however, you can find organic options made with willow extract. I find gel or liquid rooting hormone to be more effective than powder. This step is optional, but rooting hormone can help promote root growth, and I would recommend doing it. Fill one plastic cup with water and place some rooting hormone into the other one. Dip the node end of the cutting into the water and then into the rooting hormone. Tap off any excess hormone—too much can hinder the chances for successful rooting.

7. Carefully place the cutting into the hole you made in the growing medium and gently tamp the growing medium around the cutting. You can fit several cuttings into one container, but space them so the leaves don't touch one another.

8. Place the container with the cutting into a plastic bag or cover the seed staring tray with a clear plastic cover. It will keep the humidity high and hold in heat. Don't seal the bag completely because cuttings need some airflow to prevent fungal rot. You can remove the cover from the seed starting tray once a day to let the moisture escape. Keep the cuttings in a warm, sunny spot, but don't put them in full sunlight until new leaves start to appear along the stem.

9. Keep the soil slightly moist but not so wet that condensation forms on the inside of the plastic bag or seed starting tray cover until the roots form. After 2–3 weeks, you can start checking for roots by tugging gently on the cutting. When you begin to feel resistance, it means the roots have developed. At this point, you can transplant the cutting into the desired container.

You can even grow fruit trees from cuttings. The process is essentially the same, but you'll need to take either softwood or semi-hardwood cuttings from branches. Softwood cuttings are generally taken in the spring when new branches are green and no blossoms have appeared. They are flexible but will snap if you bend them hard enough. They dry out pretty quickly, so you'll need to plant them as soon as possible after taking the cuttings. Softwood cuttings usually root in about a month. Semi-hardwood cuttings are harvested in early summer when the new growth is beginning to harden and the green is starting being overtaken by bark. They should still be a little pliable, and they also dry out quickly, so you'll need to plant them as soon as possible. Semi-hardwood cuttings usually root in about 6 weeks.

Cuttings from trees should be between 6 and 12 inches (15–30 cm) long. You'll need to remove leaves from the bottom half of the cutting, and any fruit or buds should be taken off as well. Then you'll need to dip the cut end of the cutting in rooting hormone and plant it just like you would plant a cutting taken from a plant. Once the cuttings have roots that are about 1 ¼ inches (3 cm), you can transplant them into the desired containers. You'll need to grow fruit trees indoors for the first year. You can move them outside the following spring season. Of course, it takes years for trees to mature, but if you want to grow a fruit tree from scratch, growing them from cuttings is the best way to go about it. Growing fruit trees from seed can be tricky, and it's much easier to grow them from cuttings.

You can grow a lot of different plants from cuttings, including tomatoes, peppers, celery, sweet potatoes, fennel, basil, rosemary, lemon verbena, lavender, mint, and fruit trees, such as lemon, lime, apple, peach, and pear trees, and more.

When I first started out with container gardening, I started out with seeds. It's an incredible process all along, from buying packets of seeds at a garden center or online to watching the seeds sprout, grow, and get bigger and stronger, then transplanting the little seedlings into their own pots and watching the plants grow, and then eventually seeing these plants flower and fruit. You can hardly believe it—it feels magical.

Key takeaways from this chapter:

1. If you have a shaded growing space, you may be limited to leafy greens, herbs, and shade-loving plants.

2. Carefully read seed packets for information about maturity, time of year to sow, water, temperature, and light conditions.

3. Seeds are inexpensive, so you can get lots of plants for your money.

4. With seeds, you can start gardening early before spring officially starts by starting seeds indoors.

5. You can purchase seedlings from a nursery. Seedlings are sturdier and stronger, and you get to harvest them quicker than seeds. However, seedlings are more expensive than seeds and their variety can be limited.

6. Some plants don't like to be transplanted, so they need to be started directly in the desired containers, while others can be transplanted and can be started in small containers or a seed starting tray and then transplanted into larger containers.

7. You can repurpose household food packing for seed trays, such as plastic trays, containers, and egg boxes.

8. Read the seed packet carefully. If there are no details, then plant seeds to the depth that is twice of their width.

9. If you don't have a dibber to plant seeds, use a pencil.

10. Plant more than one seed per hole because not every seed will germinate.

11. Label and date planted seeds.

12. Cover seeds when they are growing with a clear plastic lid until they start to sprout. Mist them daily with a spray bottle.

13. Thin out seedlings to give more room to others to grow.

14. Try to provide as much light as possible to your seedlings to prevent them from being leggy. You can use grow lights if they don't get enough light.

15. Mist seedlings daily and fertilize them when they grow to 3 inches (7.5 cm) with an organic liquid fertilizer and then weekly after that.

16. When seedlings have 3–4 true leaves, they are ready to be transplanted into larger containers. You can transplant them into containers outside or continue growing them indoors.

17. If you have a plant that is root bound, you can gently massage it and put it into a larger pot. If roots poke out the bottom of a pot, then the plant needs a bigger pot.

18. It is fine to put soil up the stem of leggy plants when repotting, with the exception of beans and trees, because they don't like to have their stem buried and doing so can rot it.

19. You can make a dummy hole with the existing container in the new container that the plant is being transplanted into. It gives you a really good idea of size and where the soil level will be and helps make the transplant go smoothly.

20. Have a gradual transition for seedlings when you move them from indoors to outdoor containers. Move them outside for a few hours a day and gradually increase this over 10 days until they are more used to being outside.

So far throughout this book, you have learned about container gardening and the benefits and drawbacks of it. You've learned what you can grow in containers and tips to be successful with this. You've learned what tools may come in useful when doing container gardening. You've looked at specific types of containers and how to choose the right pot for different types of plants and how deep or how wide they need to be. You have learned where best to position your containers so that the plants get the right amount of sunlight or shade that they require. You will have carefully selected, mixed, and perhaps even tested the growing medium to ensure it is perfect for your container plants. You'll have chosen whether you want to grow your plants from seed or purchase seedlings or perhaps a combination of the two. The next chapter of this book is all about maintaining your garden. Taking care of your garden is super important so that all your hard work continues to pay off and your plants can thrive and produce an abundance of delicious produce.

Chapter 6: Maintaining Your Garden

This chapter will cover everything you need to know about maintaining your garden. It will look at things like how often you should water your plants and general container garden maintenance and care. This chapter will give you maintenance tips to ensure your container garden is successful. There are tips to help with watering your garden even if you're away on holiday and lots of advice on how to keep your plants and containers looking their best by pruning them and tidying up the garden and the pots, fertilizing plants, repotting plants, and looking after them in the cold winter months.

Watering

You will need to water plants in containers a lot, in fact, daily on most days because containers dry out really quickly. This will vary depending on the time of year. You will need to water your plants more during the summer months—you may need to water them twice a day if it's really hot and sunny. I love watering my container garden. I find it relaxing and enjoyable. It's a peaceful way to start the day.

People not watering their containers regularly is definitely the number one reason why container plants die. If your containers are drying out really quickly, this may be a sign that you have more plants in the container than the soil can support, so you could consider taking out some of the plants and putting them in a different container, or pruning plants back, or moving the container to somewhere where it gets slightly less direct sunlight.

Outside Tap, Water Butt, or Hose Reel

Having an outside source of water really eases the pressure of having to carry watering cans through your house. So, if you have access to an outside tap, this is a treasure! If you don't have an outside tap, you could consider getting a water butt. It's not that expensive, and it will collect lots of delicious rainwater to feed your container plants, which they'll love. It would also help you save on your water bill, so it's a win-win situation. If you don't have either of these, you could think about running a hose from a tap in your house out to the garden. Hose reels are very easy to manage. They're convenient and don't take up a lot of space but will make life much easier.

Another thing to think about regarding containers is their size. The smaller the container, the faster it will dry out. So, if you can have larger containers, they will be easier to look after. If you cover the top of your containers with a layer of either compost, shredded leaves, wood chips, or other materials (known as mulching), this will help keep the moisture in and stop water from evaporating so easily. Mulching containers will be covered later in this chapter.

Touch Soil to Determine How Moist It Is

You can purchase a wide variety of different water meters, but in all honestly, these are probably never as effective as looking at the plant yourself, placing your finger in the soil, and making a judgement call as to how dry or moist the soil is. You need to water plants regularly because otherwise they will start to wilt. When you place your finger in the soil, if the first inch (2.5 cm) you feel is dry, then it needs watering.

You can water plants until water starts flowing out of the drainage holes—this shows you have got the whole container wet. This will also leach the soil, which can help wash away any soluble salts in the soil that may accumulate from water or fertilizers.

If you are using a soilless potting mix and it starts to pull away from the edge of the pot, this is a sign that it has dried out a lot. You will need to repeatedly water this in order to fully hydrate the potting mix. It can be a good idea to place the container in a bucket or a sink with water until you can see water on the top of the container—then the potting mix is fully moist.

Built-in Reservoir

You can get containers that have a built-in reservoir to ensure your plants have a water supply. They are called self-watering pots. This reservoir may need filling on hot summer days, but it does make watering easier. You can either buy containers that already have reservoirs, or you can make your own. Reservoirs often work via a wick. You could use capillary matting or terrycloth for the wick and have a piece of material that is approximately 6 inches (15 cm) wide that goes from the reservoir into the bottom of your plant pot. When the plant needs water, it will draw it up through its roots and growing medium.

It is better to use this wick method rather than just sitting containers in a tray of water. If plants just sit in water, they can become waterlogged, and their roots may rot, which will cause them to die eventually.

Drip Irrigation System

Another technique you can use is the drip method. Take a plastic bottle and cut out the bottom. Drill tiny holes in the bottle cap. Then stick the bottle into the soil cap side down and fill it with water. You may need to experiment with the size of the holes so that the water doesn't all come pouring out too quickly or too slowly. This can be a great way to deliver water to hanging baskets too. Many gardeners, me included, love this system and suggest that it takes the guesswork out of watering.

You can also get terracotta ollas. If you place these in the soil next to plants, they will draw water from them when required. These look prettier than plastic bottles, but they cost more, so it depends on the budget you have available.

If you need to go away on holiday and don't have anyone to water your plants for you, you can set up automatic watering systems, such as a drip irrigation system with a timer, using a garden tap or water butt. You can use a container with a reservoir and connect this to a water butt. You could make a much larger reservoir (using something like an old bath) and use wicks from this to plants suspended above. All of these suggestions take a bit of setting up and some expense. But it could keep your lovely crop of fruits, vegetables, and herbs thriving if you need to go away and there's no one there to water them.

Moisture Crystals

There are various moisture crystals you can add to your potting soil or potting mix. They look like rock salt when they are dry, but when they absorb water, they take on a jellylike consistency. They act as reservoirs of moisture that plants can draw upon when the soil dries out.

These don't detract from the fact that you will need to water your containers frequently. But it will just give you a bit of a buffer until you do to help protect your plants a little.

There are some simple things you can do to help ease the load of watering your containers. A really simple tip is to purchase containers that are light colored because they won't absorb as much heat as dark-colored containers and won't dry out as quickly. Also, you can purchase non-porous containers, such as plastic or glazed terracotta ones. They won't absorb the moisture out of the soil.

Garden Maintenance and Care

If you want your plants to thrive throughout the summer months, you will need to schedule in some time to maintain your garden. As mentioned previously, one of the key tasks is watering, and this is key to the health of your plants. Watering regularly will prevent plants from being stressed, and when plants are stressed, they're more prone to disease and pests. If you don't water your plants regularly, you won't get a great harvest. It's good to check that water is flowing out the drainage holes of your containers so that the plants don't become waterlogged and their roots don't rot.

Apart from watering your plants, there are a few things you need to keep on top of, such as fertilizing and pruning your plants, turning, mulching, and tidying up your containers, removing dead/straggly plants and composting them, attracting pollinators, and repotting plants if they outgrow their pots, all of which will be covered below.

Fertilizing Plants

Once you have carefully chosen containers, filled them with the best potting soil or potting mix you're able to, and have carefully planted the seeds, it's important to maintain the plants in the best health you can. Fertilizing plants is a key part of this. Because containers dry out much quicker than plants in the garden, you will need to water them more often. As you water them, you will wash out the nutrients, so you will need to fertilize them regularly.

Plants need macronutrients to grow: nitrogen (N), phosphorus (P) and potassium (K). Nitrogen is essential for photosynthesis and amino acid production. Phosphorus is required for growth and other functions, including photosynthesis and energy transfer. Potassium is used for root growth and photosynthesis.

Usually on fertilizer you will see these key figures shown on the side to indicate how much of each of the nutrients is in there. You may see numbers like 5-5-5 or 4-6-7. These numbers refer to N-P-K ratio, and they show how much of each of the nutrients the fertilizer contains. Fertilizers that have equal amount of each of the nutrients are called balanced fertilizers, and they may have formulas like 5-5-5, or 10-10-10, and so on. For example, a fertilizer with a formula of 10-10-10 is a balanced fertilizer that has 10% nitrogen, 10% phosphorus, and 10% potassium. Balanced fertilizers work well for most plants, but for plants such as tomatoes and peppers and other fruiting plants, you can use a fertilizer with a higher K number.

There are organic and synthetic fertilizers available. Organic fertilizers are derived from plant or animal sources, while synthetic ones are manufactured from minerals and inorganic waste materials. You may notice that organic fertilizers have lower N-P-K ratios compared to synthetic ones, but that's not necessarily because they are weaker, but rather because they are slower to act.

Organic fertilizers need more time to be broken down, while synthetic ones are much faster acting and give your plants a quick boost of nutrients. But that's because synthetic fertilizers only feed the plant, while organic ones feed the soil. Organic fertilizers help improve soil structure and texture and correct imbalances in the soil. They also leave no harmful buildup of chemicals or salts, unlike synthetic fertilizers. And since they are slower acting, it's harder to overfertilize your plants.

I personally prefer using organic fertilizers, and that's what I would recommend you do too, especially if you're growing vegetables, fruits, herbs, or edible flowers, in other words, food. Organic fertilizers keep your soil healthy, and they're safe for you, your family, your pets, and the environment.

You can purchase organic fertilizers at garden centers. Organic fertilizers can be animal based (like bone meal, blood meal, fish meal, or fish emulsion), plant based (like cottonseed, alfalfa, or soybean meal, or seaweed), and there are also mineral fertilizers (like greensand or rock phosphate).

There are many different types of fertilizers for container plants, and they come in different forms. You can buy slow-release, dry (granular), and water-soluble (liquid) fertilizers.

Slow-release fertilizers come in pelleted form and are typically added to potting soil or potting mix at the time of planting. Some potting soils and mixes container fertilizer, so if yours does, do not add more fertilizer to it when planting. Slow-release fertilizers release a small amount of nutrients each time you water your plants, and most last between 60 and 120 days. There are organic options for slow-release fertilizers, which include fish meal pellets, cotton seed meal, feather meal, and alfalfa pellets. They all last for about 60 days. Alfalfa pellets also contain triacontanol, which is a hormone that promotes plant growth. You can also add compost to your potting soil or potting mix at the time of planting, and this is another organic option. You can add between 25 and 50% of compost to your potting soil or potting mix at the time of planting.

Water-soluble fertilizers are typically used as your plants grow. You just need to mix them with water and pour the mixture into your containers. Organic options for liquid fertilizers include fish meal emulsion and liquid kelp. You can apply liquid fertilizer during the growing season every 2–4 weeks, but make sure to check the instructions on the label of your product in order to avoid overfeeding the plants.

I like to use liquid seaweed fertilizer, and I water all my vegetables with it once a month. We also have a large compost pile, and I do make compost tea from time to time. Compost tea is another great organic option, and I sometimes alternate between liquid seaweed fertilizer and compost tea, and we've always had great results fertilizing our plants with this. Making compost tea is easy, and it will be covered a bit later in this chapter. Always check the soil before fertilizing, and don't fertilize your plants when the soil is dry. If the soil is dry, water your plants first, and then wait a few hours before adding fertilizer.

You can also use dry fertilizer, but I personally think that liquid fertilizer is just more convenient. To use dry fertilizer, simply sprinkle a small amount evenly over the surface of the potting soil, and then water the plant well. Make sure to use a product labeled for containers and avoid dry lawn fertilizers—they are stronger than necessary and are flushed out quickly.

Homemade Organic Fertilizers

While you can purchase organic fertilizers from garden centers, you can also make them at home from a variety of different things. If you have a compost pile, you can make compost tea, which is essentially an organic liquid fertilizer for your plants. Here's what you'll need to make compost tea:

- 3 to 4 gallons (11.4–15.2L) non-chlorinated water
- 2 to 6 cups compost
- 5-gallon (19L) bucket
- Shovel
- Strainer
- Spray bottle

Grab some compost from your compost pile with a shovel, and scoop up between 2 and 6 cups of compost. Add that to your empty bucket.

Next, you'll need some non-chlorinated water because chlorine will kill the good bacteria in your compost. You can use rainwater, or you can use tap water that has sat out for at least a day to allow the chlorine to evaporate. Add about 4 gallons (15.2L) of water to the compost in your bucket. Now you need to mix it all together. Make sure all of the compost gets completely submerged in water, and stir the mixture thoroughly so that the compost and water are combined.

Now you just need to leave the bucket in a place that's not in direct sunlight and let it sit so that the compost tea can brew. Don't leave the bucket in the sun because the heat can encourage the growth of harmful bacteria. Cold weather, rain, and snow can cause the tea to take longer to brew and can also kill beneficial microbes.

The amount of time your tea will take to brew depends on the air temperature outside. If it's above 60°F (15°C), let it sit for 12–36 hours. The lower the temperature, the longer it will take to brew. If the temperature is below 60°F (15°C), you may need to leave it for up to 72 hours. Stir the mixture once or twice a day while it's brewing.

Once the tea has finished brewing, you'll need to strain the compost from the liquid. If your compost tea isn't very dark, you don't need to dilute it. But if it's dark brown or black, you should dilute it with water to a ratio of 1:3 because it may be too strong for your plants. If you think your compost tea is not having the desired effect, you can dilute it less or even use it straight. If it's still too weak, you may need to brew the next batch longer. You can also try adding more compost to the mixture. Compost tea lasts about a week, so you'll need to use it quickly. Just use it as you would use a liquid fertilizer.

Coffee grounds are a great source of nitrogen, and you can sprinkle these directly around your plants or make a liquid mix. Simply mix 2 cups of used coffee grounds with 5 gallons (19L) of water, and steep this mixture 3–4 days before using. You can use coffee grounds every 2–4 weeks during the growing season as a liquid fertilizer. Coffee grounds work especially well for nitrogen-loving plants, such as tomatoes, peppers, pole beans, blueberries, roses, and more.

You can also make Epsom salt fertilizer by dissolving 2 tablespoons of Epsom salt per gallon (3.8L) of water. Shake the mixture vigorously, and simply substitute this solution for normal watering once a month. It works because Epsom salt is made up of magnesium and sulfate, both of which are vital plant nutrients. It works especially well for magnesium-loving plants such as roses, peppers, tomatoes, and potatoes.

Another amazing source of organic fertilizer is seaweed. If you live near a beach, you can probably just collect some from there. If you collect fresh seaweed, you can dry it, then grind it, and sprinkle it around your plants.

Plant Growth Stages

Perhaps one of the most useful things I've learned about plants over the years is how to observe the stages of plant growth. All plants follow the same basic patterns of growth on their way to maturity, and knowing at what growth stage your plants are can help you know their needs better. Plants go through the following stages during their life cycle:

- Sprout

- Seedling

- Vegetative

- Budding

- Flowering

- Ripening

Plants start their life cycle as seeds. Depending on the type of plant, seeds can take anywhere between a few days to a few weeks to germinate and sprout. All seeds need at this point is air, water, and warmth to germinate and grow into seedlings.

As roots develop, sprouts grow into seedlings. They start growing true leaves, which look like baby versions of mature leaves. The main thing that seedlings need to grow is lots of light. If you grow seedlings indoors and they become leggy because they are not getting enough sunlight, you can get grow lights to provide more light to them. This will help them grow stronger and will help prevent legginess. Seedlings also need to be watered regularly because they can't store water for very long, so you'll need to keep the soil moist. They can also benefit from fertilizing. You can fertilize seedlings when they are at least 3 inches (7.5 cm) tall with a mild dose of liquid balanced fertilizer.

When seedlings move into the vegetative stage of their life cycle, plants focus on developing sturdy stems and green, leafy growth. From this point, plants need light, water, air, nutrients, and the right temperature to grow. You'll need to water your plants regularly and fertilize them to provide them with the nutrients they need. Regarding the right temperature, plants are divided into cool-season and warm-season crops. This will be covered in detail in plant profiles in Chapter 12. When plants are in the vegetative stage, they need nitrogen, which provides the nutrients that energize the building of new cells. You can use a balanced fertilizer at all growth stages for most plants with good results. However, you may consider using a fertilizer with a higher first number (nitrogen) during the vegetative stage.

As plants grow, they transition from vegetative to budding stage when they start shifting away from green growth toward producing buds, flowers, and then fruit. In this stage, plants need more phosphorus to help encourage budding. You might consider using a fertilizer with a higher second number (phosphorus) when plants are in the budding stage.

The next stage is flowering, and this is when buds become flowers and fruiting plants begin forming fruit where flowers grew. In this stage, nitrogen becomes less important, and plants need more potassium. Potassium is important for flowering, fruit production, and overall plant health. You may consider using a fertilizer with a higher third number (potassium) when plants are in the flowering stage.

The final stage is ripening, and this is when flowers and fruit ripen and mature. In this stage, plants

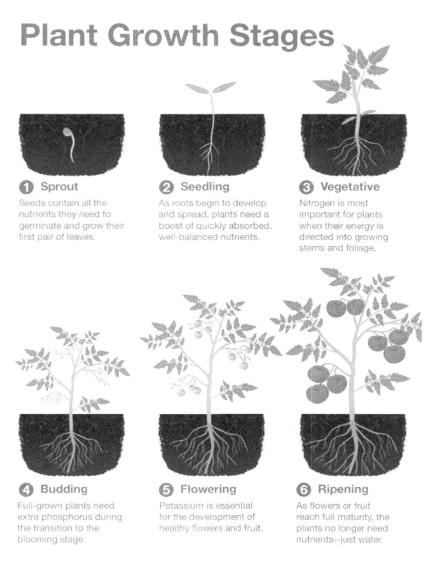

Plant Growth Stages

① Sprout
Seeds contain all the nutrients they need to germinate and grow their first pair of leaves.

② Seedling
As roots begin to develop and spread, plants need a boost of quickly absorbed, well-balanced nutrients.

③ Vegetative
Nitrogen is most important for plants when their energy is directed into growing stems and foliage.

④ Budding
Full-grown plants need extra phosphorus during the transition to the blooming stage.

⑤ Flowering
Potassium is essential for the development of healthy flowers and fruit.

⑥ Ripening
As flowers or fruit reach full maturity, the plants no longer need nutrients--just water.

no longer need added nitrogen for leafy growth because they focus their energy on finishing flowers and fruit. I would recommend that you stop fertilizing your plants in the ripening stage because when flowers and fruit are verging on full maturity, they need a week or two of just water without nutrients so that they can use up all the nutrients they have already absorbed. This process is known as flushing.

Mulching Larger Containers

Mulching means covering the soil with a thin layer of organic material. Mulching helps retain moisture in the soil, reduce weeds, keep the soil and plants' roots cool, and make containers look more attractive.

You can use different materials for mulching. Some are more aesthetically pleasing than others, while others are more functional and can add nutrients to the soil. There are two categories of mulch: organic and inorganic, and both have their advantages and disadvantages. Organic mulch is made of natural materials. It will decompose over time and add beneficial nutrients to your soil. It can reduce weeds, but it doesn't always fully block weeds. Inorganic mulch is made of synthetic materials. It can fully block weeds, and it's better at retaining moisture than organic mulch, but it won't add nutrients to the soil.

Organic mulch materials include compost, shredded leaves, shredded or chipped bark, pine needles, straw, grass clippings, newspapers, peat moss, and coconut coir. As mentioned previously, organic mulch will decompose, so it will need to be replaced after some time. But while it's decomposing, it will add nutrients to the soil as well as help improve the soil structure and drainage. The drier and woodier the mulch, the slower it will decompose and the fewer nutrients it will give to the soil.

I personally like compost using compost, shredded leaves, and coconut coir for mulching. Compost is one of the best materials for mulching. It will break down over time and provide beneficial nutrients to the soil and improve its structure and texture. Shredded leaves are great for mulching too, and they are essentially free. Coconut coir is affordable and can last you a long time. It also breaks down and improves the soil texture over time.

If you decide to use pine needles, keep in mind they can reduce the pH level of the soil and make it slightly more acidic, but usually not enough to cause any problems to plants. Also, make sure to use needles that have been dried, or they can rot and cause mold to grow on your potting soil otherwise. Most newspapers should be fine to use for mulching because they use soy-based black inks and hydrogen peroxide for bleaching pulp. But don't use glossy magazines or newspapers with colored or glossy inks because they may contain chemicals that are toxic to plants.

Inorganic mulch materials include plastic or landscape fabric and gravel or stone. Inorganic mulch materials are good at holding in moisture and blocking weeds. Since they don't decompose, they don't add any nutrients to the soil, but at the same time they don't need to be replaced as often as organic mulches.

You can't mulch small containers because you need to leave some space at the base of plants, but you can mulch larger ones. You can mulch containers that are at least a gallon (3.8 L) in volume. Don't mulch containers if you've just planted the seeds. The best time to mulch containers is when the seedlings are at least 3–5 inches (7.5–12.5 cm) tall.

To mulch your containers, simply place your chosen mulch material on the potting soil, but keep it 3 inches (7.5 cm) away from the base of the plants. Make sure the mulch is dry, and it should be in small pieces. Mulch should be placed on top of your potting soil but not in it because this will prevent your plants' roots from getting enough water, air, and nutrients they need for healthy growth. You would typically need a 2-inch (5 cm) layer of mulch for most containers. Make sure the mulch doesn't touch the leaves of your plants because this can spread diseases.

When you water your mulched containers, aim the water at the base of plants. You might need to separate the mulch from the base of the plants before watering. If you pour water directly on the mulch, it may lead to water retention and root rot. After watering your plants, you need to put the mulch back on the potting soil. You can use drip irrigation in mulched containers, and you don't need to remove the mulch when using it because it drips water into the potting soil over time and won't soak the mulch.

You should remove mulch when the growing season has ended and the plant is dormant. When mulch seems to be too dry and brittle, you'll need to remove it and replace it with fresh material. If mulch becomes too compacted and starts blocking water flow to the roots, again, you'll need to replace it. If you notice any fungi or any signs of diseases on your plants, you'll need to remove your mulch, bag it up, and dispose of it in the trash. Some pests can use mulch as shelter, and if you notice pests in mulched areas of your garden, you can turn the mulch with a hand rake or spray it with an organic pesticide. If that doesn't help, you'll need to replace it.

Deadheading, Pinching, and Pruning Potted Plants

Deadheading means getting rid of a dead flower head of a plant. When flowers look brown and shriveled or have gone floppy and brown, you can pull these flowers off, or pinch the head off, or some will require you to cut the stem with some secateurs. When you deadhead plants, they will grow fuller and produce more flowers too. They will also continue to bloom for longer because they won't be wasting energy sending it to the dead parts of the plant. Also, when you deadhead a plant, you get rid of dead parts that are taking up space, so more oxygen can circulate around the plant, and more sunlight can get to leaves when these are removed. If you have any geraniums that have died, you can save the dried leaves of these to use as potpourri around your home.

Pinching plants means removing the end of a plant just above a node (or bulge) on the stem where the leaves are attached. When pinching plants, you remove the end set of leaves or buds, and in response, the plant sends out two new branches (also known as lateral stems), which results in more leaves and flowers. Pinching encourages branching on plants. It works especially well with herbs because it allows them to produce more desirable stems and leaves. It can also help keep plants compact. By pinching stems, you force the plant to focus on regrowing lost stems rather than growing tall. You can pinch your plants once they have formed a few pairs of leaves on a stem. You don't need to pinch your plants often—most plants can benefit from one or two pinching sessions during the growing season.

Pruning is removing parts of plants, trees, or vines that are not essential to growth or production and are no longer visually pleasing. If you prune any dead, damaged, or diseased bits of plants, this will help them to be healthy. When you're pruning a shrub or a tree, it's advisable to use varying lengths when cutting to make it look more natural, and you should be cutting branches just above buds or where a branch unites with another.

It's worth checking the guidelines for plants because some plants, such as hydrangea or wisteria, prefer to be pruned in late winter or early spring, whereas other plants, like lilac, should be pruned after they have bloomed in the spring. When you prune, don't prune in the hottest part of the day. If you're pruning deciduous plants (plants drop their leaves at the end of every growing season), early spring is a good time for this because the cuts will have plenty of time to heal before winter.

If your plants have grown really well, but your containers overcrowded, and the plants don't have room to grow, then pruning the plants can help. It will do wonders for plants in containers because it will tidy the plants up, it will encourage new bits of the plants to grow, and the plants will be bushier and more compact rather than tall and straggly.

Herbs should be given a regular trim. Some herbs will grow flowers, such as basil and cilantro. When they grow flowers, this changes the leaves and how the herb tastes. It can make herbs taste bitter, so herbs are typically harvested before they flower. A really good tip is that if you trim your herbs but don't intend to use them immediately and don't want them to go to waste, you could consider either drying them or putting them into ice cubes to use when you need them. Mint can look nice when its flowering, so you could leave a bit of this to give some nice aesthetic appearance to your plants and also attract pollinators, such as bumblebees, moths, and butterflies.

Remove Dead/Straggly Plants and Compost Them

I know it can be a wrench sometimes when you notice your plants are looking past their best, but you can gently remove them, place them in a compost pile, and replace the plant with something nice looking. You want to be pleased by the appearance of your container garden, not disappointed with how it looks.

If you have geraniums or petunias, you could replace them with African daisies, spurge, or flax in the fall and add in some chrysanthemums as well. You could also decide to plant seasonal themes so that you have things like bulbs and primroses in the spring, annuals and vegetables in the summer, and things like colored kale and pansies in the fall.

Tidy Up Leaves and Clean Containers

Another thing you'll regularly need to do is sweep up the fallen leaves and flowers that have come off the plants onto the ground. You may need to clean the pots from time to time as well to keep them looking their best because they can get bits of soil on them or bits of leaves stuck to them.

If you have containers that will not be used over the winter, empty them, and clean them thoroughly so that they are ready in the spring. Do ensure to get rid of all the old potting soil because it could have pests or their larvae in it. Wash the pot out with soap, water, and a very mild bleach solution, rinse it thoroughly, and let it air dry.

During winter is the ideal time to touch up your containers. You could have plain containers that you'd like to add a splash of color to by painting them. Or maybe some pots could have a chip that you'd like to touch up. You can also seal your terracotta containers to prevent them from absorbing water from soil.

You can seal your terracotta pots with polyurethane. Some pots come already sealed and some don't need sealing. Plastic pots aren't porous, so they don't need sealing. Glazed ceramic pots are sealed with glaze. However, terracotta pots are porous and not sealed. Sealing your terracotta pots will give the same benefits as having glazed pots—less watering because the porous clay won't absorb water from soil once it's sealed.

You'll need to give your pots a good wash before sealing them. Scrub the pot with dishwashing liquid and warm water. You can use a wire brush to give it a good scrub if there's some caked-on dirt or fungus. Rinse the pot after washing and scrubbing it, and leave it to air dry completely.

Next, you'll need water or oil-based polyurethane spray or other non-toxic sealant and latex gloves. Make sure to seal your pot in a well-ventilated area. Put on the gloves and start spraying the sealant inside and outside the pot. Keep your hand moving and don't spray too long in one spot. Try to apply even coats. Leave the pot to dry. You can check the label of the product you used for drying time. Once it's completely dry, you can apply a second coat.

Once you've sealed your pot, you can paint over the sealant if you want to decorate it. Use acrylic paint and make sure to use outdoor acrylics if the pot stays outside. To paint your pot, place it upside down on a newspaper, and paint the bottom. Once it's dry, turn it over, and paint the lip and the outside. You can apply multiple coats of paint. For example, you can paint the pot a certain color and use it as a base layer, and then you can paint some designs or patterns over it. Always let a layer of paint dry completely before painting over it.

Repotting Plants That Have Outgrown Their Pots

When your plants outgrow the container they're in, you'll need to put them in a bigger container, which will give more room for their roots to grow and help the plants to thrive. If you can see your plant's roots start to poke out of the drainage holes, the plant needs to be repotted as soon as possible. You can also check if a plant is root bound by removing the plant from its pot and looking at the roots.

If you repot plants into containers that are typically two to two and a half times the size of the outgrown one, this may mean you won't have to repot them too often. When repotting a root-bound plant, try to loosen the roots by massaging them very gently before putting the plant into a new container with fresh potting mix and fertilizer.

Turning Containers

It can be a good idea to turn your containers from time to time so that all sides of your containers get as much sun and your plants don't lean trying to grow toward the sun. You can turn your containers a quarter turn every week or two if you notice your plants start leaning toward the light.

Attracting Pollinators

The majority of plants grown in containers don't need insect pollinators to produce fruit. They can be self-pollinating (tomatoes, eggplants, peppers, beans, peas), or they can use the wind to pollinate their flowers (strawberries, corn), or they are not grown for their flowers (carrots, potatoes, onions, garlic, lettuce, broccoli, cauliflower, and herbs). Plants that need insect pollinators include fruit trees, berry bushes, cucumbers, squash, pumpkins, and watermelons (although it's quite difficult to grow them in containers).

Many people think that only bees are pollinators, but that's not true. Birds and butterflies are pollinators too. Different pollinators respond to different colors. Bees prefer blue, yellow, white, and purple. Hummingbirds love red-toned blooms. Butterflies favor red and purple tones. Filling your yard with flowers in a rainbow of hues is one of the best ways to attract pollinators. Some flowers, like marigold, also help deter pests while attracting pollinators.

Like all living creatures, pollinators need water. You can leave small containers with water around your garden to help attract pollinators. If you grow herbs, you can allow them to flower. Pollinators will swarm your garden if you do this. Letting herbs flower often makes their flavor weaker, but you don't have to let all your herbs flower. Leave a plant or two to flower—this will be more than enough. Pollinators love basil, mint, oregano, dill, fennel, and rosemary flowers.

Most gardeners don't have any problems with natural pollination. However, if you decide to grow plants indoors, you may need to pollinate some of them by hand. Even if you're growing outdoors, sometimes you may notice your plants blooming profusely, but despite lots of flowers, the harvest may be meager. This usually happens due to insufficient pollination. The use of broad-spectrum pesticides and habitat loss has led to a decline in pollinator populations. As pollinator populations decline, often the necessary insects just aren't there when you need them to pollinate your plants.

Plants can be pollinated by wind, insects, or birds, and hand pollination mimics that natural process. How a plant is pollinated depends on the type of flowers they have. Self-pollinating plants have perfect or complete flowers in which both male (stamen) and female (pistil) reproductive organs are contained in the same flower. Plants with imperfect flowers have male and female flowers growing separately. Hand pollination helps transports the pollen from male flowers to female flowers when there aren't enough pollinators around.

If you need to pollinate your plants by hand, it's best to do this in the morning hours when the humidity is high, which helps activate the pollen. Self-pollinating plants typically don't need hand pollination. Just a little bit of air movement or vibration is usually sufficient. Although these plants don't usually need hand pollination, you can help them along by gently tapping the flowers or using a small brush or a cotton swab to move the pollen from the stamen to the pistil. With strawberries, hand pollination can help improve yield. You can either transfer the pollen from the stamens on the outside of the flower to the pistils in the center with your finger, or a cotton swab, or a small, fine brush.

To pollinate plants with imperfect flowers, you'll need to identify male and female flowers first and then transfer the pollen from a male to a female flower using a cotton swab or a small, fine brush. Different plants have different flowers, so I'd recommend doing some research online to see how male and female flowers look on your plants. For example, cucumber male flowers often grow in clusters, and female flowers grow singly. Male flowers usually appear first on cucumber plants, and female flowers begin at a small fruit, which makes them easier to identify. Squash male flowers have a plain stem below the flower, and female flowers have a tiny rudimentary squash below the petals.

To pollinate plants with imperfect flowers, gently peel back a petal from a male flower to uncover the male anther that carries the pollen. Use a cotton swab or a small, fine brush to pick up the pollen and apply it onto the stigma of a female flower of the same plant. You can use the same male flower to pollinate several female flowers.

Anther

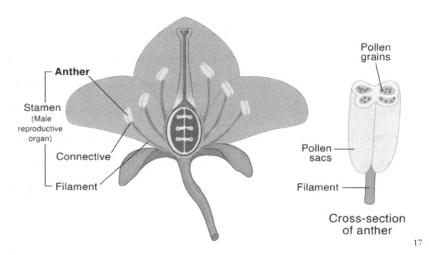

Cross-section
of anther

17

Stigma

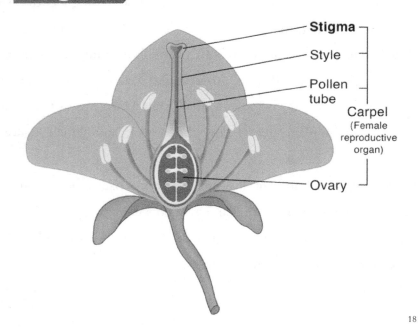

18

---

17 Image from: https://www.sciencefacts.net/anther.html
18 Image from: https://www.sciencefacts.net/stigma.html

Preventing Animals from Eating Plants

Depending on where you live and what wildlife comes into your garden, you may need to take action to protect your beloved plants. The most obvious choice is putting up a fence, especially if there are large animals, such as deer, getting into your garden. Of course, fencing your whole lot is not always feasible or desirable, and motivated critters can find openings in any fence. But putting up a fence is an effective way to stop unwanted critters from getting into your garden.

If you have smaller critters, such as rabbits, getting into your garden, you can put your pots high up on tables to repel them. You could consider moving the containers into a garage overnight if they are being frequently eaten.

You can spray your plants with liquids that have an offensive odor or taste, and this is perhaps the least expensive way to repel critters. There are commercial products, such as Deer-Off (based on eggs, hot peppers, and garlic) and Plantskydd (a blood-meal solution), that you can spray directly on plants to make them unpalatable. There are also products that contain predator scents, such as coyote urine, that can be placed strategically around the yard.

You can make a homemade spray that's quite effective in my experience. Mix 1 ounce (30 ml) of hot pepper sauce (the hotter the better), 4 drops of dish soap, and 1 cup of marigold leaves or 5 cloves of garlic. Put all the ingredients in a blender, add a cup or two of water, and mix until smooth. Strain the mixture to remove any solids and put it in a spray bottle. Spray the mixture on your plants once a week, and reapply it after every rain. Make sure to label the bottle, and store it in the fridge.

Critters can often be kept at bay with scare tactics—usually a surprise burst of water or a loud noise works well. You can buy a scarecrow with a motion detector and a sprinkler that sprays water when critters cross its path. Placement is important with such products, so you might need to observe where critters come from. If you have a dog—that's great. Dogs are good at scaring away various critters.

You can also try adding plants that animals don't like—these are usually bitter-tasting or aromatic plants that have a strong fragrance. Marigolds don't need much maintenance, and they can help repel critters. Herbs, such as mint and lavender, can also help keep pests and critters away due to their pungent odor.

Caring for Plants During Winter

If you have the room, it can be a good idea to bring plants inside your house over the winter. You can cut them back to half their size, and they will produce new shoots. Then in the spring, you can put the containers back outside when it becomes warm again.

Hardy perennials, trees, and shrubs will not be able to survive if their roots become completely frozen. With shrubs and trees, it's a good idea to wrap some chicken wire around the pots and stuff this with mulch and straw and then place them in a garage or a basement over the winter so that these plants are not killed off in the freezing conditions.

If you have terracotta or ceramic pots, these can crack during the winter. You can store empty pots that have been cleaned and sanitized in places like a garage, a cellar, or a shed to prevent these from cracking in the winter.

Lighting for Indoor Plants

If you're wondering whether your plants that you move indoors over the winter will get enough light, or perhaps you want to grow plants in containers indoors, the good news is that most plants do just fine indoors with whatever natural light they get. However, some sun-loving plants may struggle indoors, especially if your home doesn't get a lot of natural light. When growing indoors, it's important to match the natural sunlight requirements for your plants. This can easily be done by using grow lights.

Outdoor gardens require 6–8 hours of direct sunlight per day. If your plants don't get enough natural light indoors, you can provide them with more light with grow lights. Artificial lighting provided by grow lights should imitate the direct and indirect lighting requirements for your plants. Different plants have different needs, but typically your plants would need 8–10 hours of artificial light per day if they are getting some sunlight, and up to 16 hours if they don't get any sunlight.

Choosing the right grow lights for your plants can be a daunting task, as there are a lot of different options on the market. Some grow lights may be better or more efficient depending on the types of plants you're growing. The pros and cons of different grow lights will be covered below to help you choose the right grow lights for your plants.

Different Types of Grow Lights

All grow lights have 4 different components: bulbs, a reflector hood, a remote ballast, and a timer. Let's take a closer look at each of these components.

Bulbs

The most common types of bulbs in grow lights are LED, fluorescent, metal halide (MH), and high-pressure sodium (HPS).

LED grow lights are one of the newest forms of artificial lighting for plants. They are one of the most energy-efficient types of lighting. Plants need different light spectrums at different growth stages, and some LED grow lights (full-spectrum or RGB LEDs) can provide different light spectrums, which makes them really versatile.

Fluorescent grow lights give off a blue hue, and they are great for starting seeds and the beginning stages of seedlings. They have a low heat output, which allows seeds to grow without getting burned or drying out. They also work well for growing salad greens and flowers.

Metal Halide (MH) grow lights are solid all-around lights. They provide the blue/white light spectrum, and they imitate sunlight during the summer months. They are mainly used for plants that have just finished sprouting and are now entering the growing or vegging stage. They also work well for long-day plants that require more light.

High-Pressure Sodium (HPS) grow lights give off an orangey-red hue, imitating the warmer colors of fall, and they work best for flowering and fruiting stages of your plants. Typically, you would use MH lights when your vegetables and fruits are starting to grow, and you would switch to HPS lights when your plants start flowering.

MH and HPS grow lights are a popular choice for many indoor growers. They are cheaper than LEDs, but they are less energy-efficient, they generate a lot of heat, plus they lose their effectiveness over time and their lifespan is shorter, so they need to be replaced more often (usually every year). Even though the initial expense is higher when buying LED grow lights, they can last for years, unlike MH or HPS grow lights, which may only last a few seasons. Generally, full-spectrum LED grow lights are your best bet because they are highly versatile, energy efficient, and produce balanced white light that is similar to sunlight plants get in nature.

Light Fixture

Light fixture is the main structure of the lights. It holds the bulbs, sockets, electrical wires and other components.

Reflector Hood

Reflector hood is a reflective casing around the bulb. It reflects the light down onto the plants at multiple angles, which helps increase the effectiveness of the bulbs and distribute the light more evenly.

Remote Ballast

The ballast is the power box that powers the grow lights. Ballasts can be sold as a part of the lamp assembly, but these can be too hot and heavy. Remote ballasts work much better for home systems. They are usually the most expensive element of the lighting system, so make sure to keep your remote ballast off the ground so that it never gets wet in case of a flood. I would recommend buying the ballast as a set with the bulbs because their wattage must match.

Timer

Plants need darkness just as much as they need light, so it's important to get a timer for your grow lights. It should be heavy-duty and grounded, and timers can be either manual or digital.

Grow Lights Wattage

A rule of thumb is to have 20–40 watts per square foot of grow space. This means a 1000-watt LED grow light can cover 25–50 square feet (2.3–4.6 sq m). The efficiency of your lighting system is the key to increasing the wattage. LED grow lights are the most efficient lights, and a 500-watt LED light can provide equivalent ratings to a 1000-watt MH or HPS light.

Distance to Plants

How high you should have your grow lights above your plants depends on the type of lights you have. I'd suggest following the height recommendations provided by the light manufacturer. However, if that information isn't provided, fluorescent grow lights should be kept 2–3 inches (5–7.5 cm) above plants, and LED grow lights should be at least a foot (30 cm) above. MH lights also need to be mounted at least a foot (30 cm) above plants, and HPS lights need to be 12–18 inches (30–45 cm) above plants. The distance to plants also depends on the wattage of your grow lights. The more powerful lights you have, the further they'll need to be from plants. You'll need to move your grow lights away from plants as they grow.

Maintaining my container garden is now second nature to me, and I definitely find it more of a therapeutic experience rather than a chore. I absolutely love going out first thing in the morning on a beautiful spring or summer day to take a look at how all the plants are doing. I adore how the container garden looks with the incredible array of brightly colored glazed terracotta pots—it's absolutely stunning. They're filled with a wide variety of plants with an abundance of brightly colored fresh produce—peppers, tomatoes, strawberries, blueberries, cucamelons, flowers, and much more. I get enormous pleasure from looking at the plants and tending to them. I enjoy watering and fertilizing the plants and like to see how much perkier the plants look after a good feed. I will turn containers that can be turned so that the plants in them grow evenly and don't curve toward the sun. Once you get into your own gardening routine, it will become second nature to you to keep an eye on the health of your plants and notice any yellowing or wilting leaves, check for any signs of pests and diseases, and deal with it swiftly if you spot this.

When I am tending to my container garden, I feel that this is my time. Just for me and my plants. It's my time to wind down, relax, and be calm. In the morning, I do this before the family is up and often sit on the bench out there admiring the view with a cup of coffee before wandering among all the containers. Plants don't take up a lot of time and effort, and they give infinitely more back with the lovely vegetables and fruits they produce. Often in the morning, as I cast my eyes over the containers, I take stock of the vegetables and fruits that are ready to be harvested later that day, and this will give me plenty of inspiration for how we could use them in delicious meals and desserts.

Key takeaways from this chapter:

1. You can use things like outside taps, water butts, or a hose reel to help water your containers.

2. Water containers daily (sometimes twice a day in the hot summer months).

3. Stick your finger 1 inch (2.5 cm) deep into the soil to feel the moisture. If it is dry, water it. If it feels moist, wait.

4. Ensure water flows out of the drainage holes so that your plants don't become waterlogged and their roots don't rot.

5. Using light-colored, non-porous containers will help keep the moisture in, so you won't have to water your containers as often.

6. Larger containers are easier to keep moist than smaller ones.

7. Mulch the top of containers to help keep in moisture, keep the soil and plants' roots cool, and reduce weeds.

8. Consider using drip irrigation systems with plastic bottles, or you can place terracotta ollas next to plants to help keep the soil moist.

9. Turn your containers to make sure all plants get a good amount of sunlight.

10. Deadhead, pinch, and prune plants so that they bloom for longer.

11. Check pruning guidelines for when to prune plants and don't prune at the hottest part of the day.

12. Remove dead or dying plants and replace them with new plants.

13. Fertilize plants often to give them nutrients.

14. You can add compost as fertilizer at the time of planting, and you can also make compost tea from it and use it as a liquid organic fertilizer.

15. Deter animals from eating your plants.

16. Repot plants when they become too large for their containers.

17. Bring plants indoors over winter to stop pots from cracking and plants from freezing and dying.

18. During the winter is a great time to spruce up pots and get them ready for spring.

The next chapter will move on to looking at pest control and dealing with diseases. While hopefully this won't happen often, it is something to be aware of when you do your daily garden maintenance. You can get into the process of checking for pests and looking for signs of these on leaves or stems. You will also learn what symptoms to look out for if your plants have a disease. The next chapter will cover preventative measures you can take to prevent pests and diseases and also things you can do to tackle these and nip them in the bud to get rid of pests or diseases and get your plants back to health without this spreading and ruining all your crop.

Chapter 7: Pest Control and Dealing with Diseases

In this chapter, we will look at the types of pests that could attack your plants, how to spot them, how to prevent pest infestations, and how to get rid of them swiftly to prevent them from spreading all over your garden. The chapter will also look at different diseases that could impact your plants, the signs and symptoms to look out for, and what you can do to prevent and resolve these. Some insects are good for your garden, and this chapter will cover the ones you should be glad to see too.

You should definitely be checking your plants for pests a couple of times a week. Things you should be looking out for include nibbled leaves, leaves where you can see the skeleton of the leaf showing, any flower buds missing, and leaves that have pock marks on them. It's then a good idea to thoroughly research what type of pest you have so that you can be sure you're treating them in the right way. Sometimes you can remove pests by hand and then wash and wipe the plant thoroughly. Other times, you may need some organic pest control.

You may wonder where the pests could come from. They could come from the nursery where you bought the plant. Or it could be pests that were in the soil that you may have reused or soil from the garden. If a fruit or a vegetable has become infected by a pest, it could spread from there. If you've used a container from a previous growing session and it hasn't been cleaned out properly, pests can come from that. Pests do spread quickly and can cause a lot of damage to your plants, so it's important to get rid of them as soon as possible.

If a plant has been decimated by pests, then sometimes the best approach can be to just pull up the plant and dispose of it. Doing this will help remove pests from your garden and won't allow them to spread and destroy any other plants.

Common Garden Pests

Aphids

Aphids are a common garden pest. They are small, 1/16- to 1/8-inch-long (2–4 mm), pear-shaped, soft-bodied insects. They can be a variety of different colors, including green, black, red, yellow, brown, or gray. They attack a lot of different plants, including tomatoes, lettuce, kale,

and cabbage, and they especially love fruit trees and flowering plants. They suck the sap out of stems and new leaves. There are things you can do to prevent aphids and stop them from attacking your plants.

Do regularly check your plants to ensure they don't have aphids. If your plants ever look yellow or brown or if they curl or wilt, do check to ensure there are no aphids on your plants. Because aphids leave behind honeydew (a sugary liquid that is released by pests as they eat your plants), this can cause sooty mold on your plants. If your container garden also has ants, this will exacerbate the aphid issue because ants and aphids work hand in hand. Ants will protect aphids because ants like honeydew. A great biological control to deal with aphids is to stop ants first, and this will be discussed in the next section of this chapter that covers dealing with pests.[19]

---

[19] Image from: http://www.balconycontainergardening.com/wildlife/633-tips-for-aphid-control

Ants

Ants like containers because they can find food, water, and shelter in them. If you have other pests, such as aphids, soft scales, mealybugs and whiteflies, ants love them because all these pests produce honeydew, which is one of their favorite things to eat. Ants often protect these pests from predators

and parasites so that they can continue to produce honeydew. Dealing with ants can help reduce the abundance of honeydew-producing pests.[20]

Fungus Gnats

Fungus gnats are small and quite difficult to see, but you may see them move over the soil in your containers. They are very small and look gray or black in color with see-through wings.

They can lay eggs in the soil, and when their larvae hatch, these can eat the roots of your plants. Fungus gnats are attracted to the moisture of potting soil, and they will lay eggs on the soil surface.

When the eggs turn into larvae, they burrow into the soil and feed on decaying plant material. Fungus gnats don't attack plants and don't bite humans, but their larvae can badly affect plants'

---

[20]   Image from: https://www.gardeningknowhow.com/plant-problems/pests/insects/ants-in-flower-pots.htm

roots, and they may spread Pythium, which can cause damping off in seedlings. Getting rid of fungus gnats larvae will be covered in the next section of this chapter.

You can look for fungus gnat damage by spotting them on top of your soil and looking for lower leaves looking yellow or dropping off. The entire plant could wilt if it's young and the root system has been damaged.[21]

Leaf Miners

You can often tell that your plants have leaf miners if you see trails on the leaves. The trails wind round and may look silver or beige. They appear on shrubs, vegetables, fruit trees, bushes, and perennials. These are caused by the larvae of a small dark fly. The female fly will make little cuts in the leaf surface and lay her eggs there, and the larvae will tunnel inside the leaf just under the surface. They will feed there, and after 2–3 weeks they'll emerge as adults.

This mostly just makes the leaves of your plants look unpleasant, but if there's a lot of damage to leaves, then the plant could become weak and even die. One of the most effective ways to get rid of this is to remove the infected leaves as soon as you see the trails and dispose of them. Don't add these leaves to compost. Bag them up and dispose of them in the trash.

---

[21] Image from: https://www.almanac.com/pest/fungus-gnats

Mealybugs

Mealybugs look like white, cottony masses that appear on the leaves, stems, and fruit of plants. They have a sucking mouthpart that draws sap out of plants. Plants will turn yellow, curl, and become weak. Mealybugs produce honeydew, which can encourage sooty mold to grow and attract ants. They attack a lot of different plants, including asparagus, beans, beets, cabbage, cucumbers, lettuce, pepper, pumpkins, tomatoes, and more.

Pill Bugs

There are a number of ways to get rid of pill bugs, and one way is to ensure you have food for them that is away from your container garden. For example, you could have a compost pile out of the way that contains decomposing plants, grass clippings, leftover fruit rinds, corn cobs, and so on, and this should keep the pill bugs happy and away from your containers. Pill bugs aren't really going to harm your plants, so if you see some near the containers, you shouldn't worry too

---

22 Image from Wallygrow.com: https://wallygrow.com/blogs/feature/how-to-get-rid-of-mealybug-on-houseplants

much about it. If you saw masses of them, then you may need to do something about it. There are a few things you can do to get rid of pill bugs.

Ensure that the area near the containers is kept clean and tidy. If you have debris from leaves, grass clippings, pieces of wood, or soil, this will attract them. Ensure that you use good quality potting soil that drains well because pill bugs like to nest in moist soil. If you water your plants in the morning, then the soil has a chance to absorb the moisture, and when the sun comes out, it will certainly dry the surface of the soil in your container.

A top tip is that you can put a toilet paper tube around seedlings, and this would stop pill bugs from reaching your plants. If you're growing heavy vegetables or fruits that may touch the soil allowing pill bugs to get to them, you could provide support for the plants by using a cage or a stake to keep them off the soil. You can even repurpose old t-shirts to make a sling for melons. If you place containers on concrete, this may discourage pill bugs because it's not as likely that water or dampness will accumulate there. Another option would be to grow plants in hanging baskets. They'll be well off the ground, and pill bugs won't reach them.

23

---

23 Image from: https://www.thoughtco.com/fascinating-facts-about-pillbugs-4165294

Root-Knot Nematodes

Nematodes are parasite worms that burrow into roots, and this stops the roots from absorbing the necessary water and nutrients. You can check the roots of your plants by pulling out one plant and looking at the roots to see if it has little balls or knots in the roots. To treat nematodes, once you have harvested the crop, you can bring the roots out into the sun, and direct sunlight will kill nematodes. French marigolds' roots release a chemical that is toxic to nematodes, so you can plant French marigolds near plants with nematodes.

Spider Mites

Spider mites are a common pest. They're extremely small, they have 8 legs, and they can be red, green, yellow, or brown. They emerge in the spring and eat plants, which makes the plants weak and susceptible to diseases. They attack a lot of different plants, but they're especially attracted to strawberries, tomatoes, melons, and fruit trees. A female spider mite can lay hundreds of eggs and infestations grow really quickly. Definitely look under the leaves of plants because they will hide there.

If the infestation is really bad, get rid of the infested leaves by removing them and placing in a sealed plastic bag and dispose of them in garbage. Don't add these infected leaves to your compost because the infestation could spread.

Springtails

Springtails love moisture, and they swarm together in clouds that you can see in the air. They can be brown, gray, black, or white. They like wet soil, rotting straw, decaying leaves, and other damp organic matter. They feed on mold, fungi, and algae. They are mostly a nuisance pest and won't damage plants or harm people or pets. They will chew roots in the soil where they're located, which can inhibit plant hardiness, but they rarely do significant damage. If the soil dries out, they will likely find a new home.[24]

Thrips

Thrips are small insects—they are usually 2 millimeters in length. When they're young, they are pale yellow. When they're adults, they are brown or black. In order to know whether you have thrips, you can hang sticky traps near your plants. If leaves are looking dull or have a silver mottling, you may have thrips. If you look really close at the leaf, you may see little black dots on it.

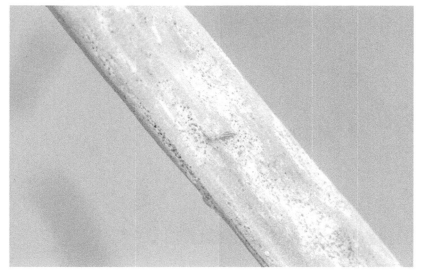

Certain plants tend to get thrips more often, and

---

[24] Image from: https://www.planetnatural.com/pest-problem-solver/houseplant-pests/springtail-control/

these include onions, peas, tomatoes, cucumbers, beans, carrots, and many flowers, especially gladioli and roses. Thrips like dry and hot conditions, so if you increase humidity around your plants, this can discourage them. If you get rid of dead leaves and fallen flowers off plants, this can discourage thrips too.[25]

Whiteflies

White flies are sap-sucking pests, and they target vegetables and ornamental plants. They produce honeydew, which can lead to sooty black mold and attract ants. Look for yellow leaves and white ovals under leaves which may be whitefly eggs.[26]

[25] Image from: https://www.gardenersworld.com/how-to/solve-problems/thrips/
[26] Image from: https://www.naplesgarden.org/container-gardening-bugs-friends-or-foes/

Dealing with Pests

General advice to keep plants free from pests is to inspect any plants you buy before bringing them home to your container garden to ensure they're free from pests. Keep your plants healthy with regular watering and fertilizing. This will keep them strong and less susceptible to pests and diseases. Keep your container garden as clean as possible, and get rid of fallen leaves and debris where pests can gather. Some pests like dry conditions (spider mites), whereas other pests like moist conditions (pill bugs), so depending on what pests you have, try to increase or decrease moisture accordingly. Always use the best quality potting soil you can to avoid soilborne pests.

I would advise you to use organic pest control, especially if you're growing vegetables and fruits that you then intend to eat. Using organic pesticides is less damaging to the soil and environment rather than using chemical pesticides. Organic methods of pest control do work and can even be more effective than chemical pesticides in some cases.

You can purchase organic pesticides from garden centers to help control pests. Make sure to check the packaging carefully to make sure the spray you're purchasing is organic. They will contain bacillus, which is a bacterium. They may have neem oil and copper in them too. You can also make your own organic pesticides from household products or plants.

Organic Pesticides/Sprays

It is advisable to spray pesticides on a small part of a plant rather than the whole thing at first just to check it doesn't damage it. Also, don't spray pesticides in really hot sun because this can burn plants.

Neem Oil Spray

Neem oil is typically used when you have an infestation, but you can spray your plants with neem oil solution every 2–3 weeks as a preventative measure. This is good to get rid of soft-bodied insects, such as aphids, fungus gnats, thrips, whiteflies, spider mites, springtails, and mealybugs. Neem oil also works well for treating leaf miners. Pests won't lay eggs after being sprayed, and they will eat less and grow more slowly. Neem oil spray would sadly work on beneficial insects too, so you could spray early in the morning or late in the afternoon, and then cover with a row cover to stop honeybees from being affected. It can also prevent powdery mildew. It does have quite a strong smell. Simply follow the instructions on the label, make a spray, and spray your plants every 3–4 days until pests are gone, and reapply the solution after it rains.

Insecticidal Soap

You can buy insecticidal soap or make homemade insecticidal soap by mixing 1 tablespoon of liquid soap with a quart (0.95L) of water. Just like neem oil, insecticidal soap works well against soft-bodied insects. Simply follow the instructions on the label, make a spray, and use it to spray your plants once or twice a week until pests are gone.

Chili Pepper Spray

This spray is effective against most insects and pests attacking your plants. Mix half a cup of chopped hot peppers, 2 cups of water, and 2 tablespoons of dish soap (with no bleach). Let this sit overnight, strain it, then place in a spray bottle, and spray on plants. Spray your plants every 3–4 days until the infestation is gone. Reapply the spray after it rains.

Garlic Spray

This is great for getting rid of pest and insect infestations. You can make this out of a head of garlic, a tablespoon of dish soap (with no bleach), 2 tablespoons of vegetable oil, and 2 cups of water. Mix the ingredients together, and allow the mixture to sit overnight. Then put it into a spray bottle, and use on infected plants. Garlic has fungicidal effects and is good for getting rid of aphids, squash bugs, whiteflies, and other pests. Spray your plants every 3–4 days until pests are gone. Reapply the spray after it rains.

Oil Spray

This solution is super easy to make. It works great against aphids, mealybugs, mites, leaf miners, whiteflies, and beetle larvae. Simply mix a tablespoon of vegetable oil, 2 tablespoons of baking soda, 1 teaspoon of dish soap, and 2 quarts (1.9 L) of water, put the mixture into a spray bottle, and spray on affected plants. Spray as necessary until pests are gone.

Soap Spray

This will help get rid of pests and insects and will keep your plants safe. Soap spray works well against aphids, whiteflies, mealybugs, thrips, spider mites, and other soft-bodied pests and insects. It doesn't work well against larger insects, such as caterpillars, sawflies, and beetle larvae, however. You can dilute 2 teaspoons of dish soap with a quart (0.95 L) of water. The insects become dehydrated and die. You will need to spray your plants every 4–7 days until pests are gone, and don't forget to reapply after it rains.

Rubbing Alcohol Spray

Rubbing alcohol spray can help get rid of pests. Mix 1 part 70% rubbing alcohol with 9 parts water, and spray your plants with this every 3–4 days until the infestation is gone.

Apart from sprays, there are other organic methods to deal with pests:

Water

You can spray your plants with a hose to remove pests like aphids, spider mites, and thrips, but don't blast your plants because this can damage them.

Diatomaceous Earth (DE)

You can use a shaker to pest-proof plants with this powder. This absorbs the moisture from the bodies of insects and pests. It will work against slugs, aphids, caterpillars, and thrips. It will, however, also kill beneficial insects, so be careful with it. You can put it on the soil around your plants. If you have any leaves that show signs of an infestation, then you can put it underneath the leaves.

Release or Attract Beneficial Insects to Your Garden

You can buy predatory beneficial insects, such as ladybugs (ladybirds) and lacewings, from garden centers or online and then release them into your garden, and they will eat pests, such as aphids, spider mites, mealybugs, whiteflies, thrips, and others. However, they will likely disperse after eliminating the pests. You can make them stay and also attract more beneficial insects by planting certain plants and providing water for them. If you want to attract beneficial insects that will eat pests to your garden, then planting some marigolds, yarrow, cosmos, and dill will bring lots of beneficial insects to your garden. You can also leave small trays with water around your garden, and this will help attract beneficial insects too.

Remove Pests by Hand

You can pick off insects and pests by hand. This is easy to do this with snails, slugs, caterpillars, and squash bugs. Most insects won't harm you, but you can wear rubber gloves just in case. You will need to kill the insects or place them in a plastic bag or container with a lid that they can't escape from. Keeping your garden clean also helps prevent pests. You can clear away any dropped or fallen leaves or fruits and put them into the compost pile if they are not diseased.

Nip Off Infected or Infested Leaves and Plants' Parts

One of the best organic prevention and control methods for pests and diseases is to regularly inspect your plants and physically remove any pests or diseased areas. You can nip off infected or infested leaves or buds or pull up infected crops. You can prune off parts of plants that look like they have disease or pests.

Dealing with Ants

If you have ants in containers, get a bucket or a tub that is larger than the container and place the container inside the bucket or tub. Make up a water solution that is two tablespoons of insecticidal soap per quart of water. Fill up the bucket or tub until the solution just covers the surface of the potting soil and leave it to soak for 20 minutes.

If you spot a lot of ants in your garden and they continue to infest your containers, try to find ant trails and follow them to see where they lead you. Ant trails usually lead to ant mounds, where all the ants live alongside their queen ant. You need to kill the queen ant to destroy a colony. You can pour boiling water onto the mound, and it may reach the queen through the tunnels. However, it may sometimes not work because even boiling water cools down quickly on contact with earth, or the queen may be deeper underground, and the water might not reach her.

Using borax is a much more effective way of dealing with ants. Mix ½ cup sugar, 1.5 tablespoons of borax, and 1.5 cups of water. Soak some cotton balls in the mixture, and put them in places where you see lots of ants. Sugar will attract the ants, and they will take borax to their home, where they will eat it later. Eating borax will kill the ants.

Dealing with Fungus Gnats Larvae

To get rid of fungus gnats larvae, you'll need to make a neem oil soil soak. Add 2 tablespoons of neem oil and 1 teaspoon of liquid dish soap to a gallon (3.8L) of water. When it's time to water, water your plants like you normally would, but with this solution instead of water. You can pour a cup of this solution into the soil to see that the plant doesn't have any negative reactions.

Wash Plants Before Bringing Them Indoors

One really useful tip is to shower the plants thoroughly if you bring your containers in the house over the winter months to wash off any pests that could spread to your indoor plants.

Dealing with Diseases

Diseases in plants are usually caused by either fungi, bacteria, or viruses. If you have rain showers and warm temperatures, look for fungal and bacterial diseases. In the summer, look for viral diseases. Nematodes love warm weather but can impact the roots of plants all year round.

Because you'll be watering and maintaining your garden on a daily basis, it's generally quite easy to spot if your plants are suffering from any diseases. You should try to tackle these swiftly before they become a big issue and spread.

This has been discussed earlier in the book, but it's never a good idea to reuse potting soil, and this is definitely the case if any plants have ever shown signs of diseases. Soil can have eggs or larvae in it that you may not be able to see. You should always thoroughly clean out containers before you reuse them. Make sure that there's no soil left in them. Wash them with soapy water and a mild bleach solution, rinse them thoroughly, and leave them to air dry.

If you buy plants from a nursery, check that they're healthy. Ensure your plants have enough water, sunlight, and enough space for air to flow around them. If you identify any infected plants, remove them and dispose of them in a plastic bag in the trash. Never put infected plants in a compost pile.

If you have been working with diseased plants, then ensure you wash your hands, tools, and gardening gloves before handling any other plants so that you don't spread diseases. If you don't live in a tropical area but have purchased tropical plants, these may be more prone to diseases because they're not native to the area and haven't built up resistance to local garden pests.

Fungal Diseases

If you see that your plants are wilting, or you have noticed spots on your plants' leaves, or if you can see rotten plant stems, this could be due to a fungal disease. Fungi thrive in dark and damp conditions, so too much rainfall can cause fungal diseases in plants. To prevent fungal diseases from occurring, water your plants at the base and make sure that plenty of air can circulate around your plants and that all your plants get a good amount of sunlight.

Fungicides are used to treat fungal diseases, although not all diseases can be treated by fungicides. You can purchase organic fungicides, such as neem oil, horticultural oil, copper, sulfur, bicarbonates, and others, from garden centers. Keep in mind that neem oil fungicides also affect beneficial insects, so try to use them in the evening when bees are not active. You can also make homemade organic fungicides with baking soda or apple cider vinegar.

To make fungicide with baking soda, mix 4 teaspoons of baking soda and 1 teaspoon of mild soap with a gallon (3.8L) of water. This fungicide recipe works especially well for stopping powdery mildew. Mix all the ingredients together, and put the mixture into a spray bottle. Spray all infected leaves top and bottom and make sure to cover all the leaves with a thick layer of the mixture so that it drips off the leaves. It can be a good idea to spray the entire plant and not just infected leaves because fungus could be hiding where you can't see it.

To make apple cider vinegar fungicide, mix 4 tablespoons of apple cider vinegar with a gallon (3.8L) of water. This simple recipe has helped me save dozens, if not hundreds, of plants. Try to spray this mixture early in the day so that the sun and acid don't burn your plants. This also works well as a preventative spray. You can spray it every 2–3 weeks just in case.

You can also mix a quart (0.95L) of warm water, a teaspoon of mouthwash, and 1 tablespoon of hydrogen peroxide to make another good homemade fungicide. Mix all the ingredients together, and spray your plants until the fungus is gone.

Below you will find a list of fungal diseases and their symptoms:

Anthracnose

This fungal disease attacks tree leaves and garden vegetables, including beans, tomatoes, cucumbers, spinach, and watermelons. It is caused by a fungus and cool, wet weather. If your plants have anthracnose, their leaves will have black, tan, or red spots as well as lesions, and the leaves may become yellow and drop off. This is a fungal disease that tends to happen in late spring and early summer. Remove infected leaves and also collect and destroy any fallen leaves. Thin your plants so that air can circulate around them. You can spray the leaves with a copper or neem oil fungicide too.

---

[27] Image from: https://www.gardentech.com/disease/anthracnose

Black Spot

Black spot displays itself as black spots on leaves that go yellow and then die. If plants are in the shade and too close together, this can cause this fungal disease. To prevent black spot, ensure your plants have plenty of space so that air can circulate around them. Also, make sure you water your plants at the base, get rid of infected leaves, and spray them with a sulfur, copper, or neem oil fungicide if you notice this. Homemade baking soda fungicide works well against black spot too.[28]

Blight

Blight refers to a specific symptom affecting plants in response to infection by a pathogenic organism. It is caused by fungi, which survive on infected plants or in plant debris. This can impact tomatoes, potatoes, and eggplants. There will be dark spots at the soil level of plants that will climb up toward the leaves of plants. If your plants have blight, act quickly to prevent it from spreading. Remove all affected leaves and burn them or put them in a plastic bag and dispose of them in the trash.

---

[28] Image from: https://www.gardentech.com/disease/black-spot

Blight is difficult to treat once it's established, but you can spray your plants with a copper fungicide in early stages of the disease.[29]

Damping Off

This is a soilborne fungal disease that kills seedlings. Their stems and roots will rot if they have damping off, and healthy-looking seedlings can just keel over and die. It mostly happens when starting seeds indoors. There is no cure for plants that already have damping off. However, you can reduce the chances of it happening it by starting seeds in fresh, soilless seed starting mix. Having proper ventilation also helps avoid damping off. A small fan or simply cracking the lid of your seed starting tray will suffice.

Downy Mildew

Downy mildew is an umbrella term for a large number of plant diseases. It is caused by a fungus-like organism called oomycetes or water molds. By the time plants show symptoms, it is already too late, so prevention is key.

This disease likes damp and cold conditions. It spreads through air and water splashing soil onto plants. Different plants can have different symptoms; however, one common symptom is yellow spots on the upper leaf surface between the leaf veins. These spots spread everywhere except the veins and eventually turn brown. Plants cannot photosynthesize on these yellow or brown spots, and when the leaf becomes totally brown, it drops. If a plant loses too many leaves, it will die.[30]

---

[29] Image from: https://www.planetnatural.com/pest-problem-solver/plant-disease/early-blight/
[30] Image from: https://www.planetnatural.com/pest-problem-solver/plant-disease/downy-mildew/

Preventing downy mildew is much easier than controlling it. Water your plants at the base and make sure they have good air circulation around them. Downy mildew spores overwinter in plant debris. After your crops are done, rake up all leaves and plant debris and dispose of them to help prevent the disease.

If your plants are seriously damaged, remove them and dispose of them in the trash. You can use copper or neem oil fungicides to control downy mildew in early stages. Homemade baking soda fungicide works well against downy mildew too.

Gray Mold

This fungal disease is also known as botrytis blight. If your plants or their fruit appear to be misshapen and have gray fungal spores, this may be due to gray mold. Gray mold causes a dark brown to black blight of flowers, buds, leaves, and stems. Wounded and old plant tissue and flowers are easily infected by gray mold. Gray mold thrives in cool and wet conditions. However, many flowering plants can recover from gray mold when warm, dry conditions return.

The best way to prevent gray mold is to space out plants so that they have good air circulation around them and can dry out after rain or watering. You need to remove infected fruit, flowers, stems, or leaves from the plant and dispose of them, and if need be, thin out the plants so that plenty of air can circulate around them. You can use fungicides to control gray mold. Mycostop is an organic fungicide that works well against gray mold.[31]

---

[31] Image from: https://www.planetnatural.com/pest-problem-solver/plant-disease/gray-mold/

Powdery Mildew

Powdery mildew is a fungal disease that affects a wide variety of plants. There are many different species of powdery mildew, and each species attacks different plants. Plants that are

commonly affected by powdery mildew include cucurbits (squash, pumpkins, cucumbers, melons), nightshades (tomatoes, eggplants, peppers), legumes (beans, peas), and roses.

Plants infected with powdery mildew look as if they have been dusted with flour. This disease usually starts off as circular, powdery white spots, which can appear on leaves, stems, and sometimes fruit. It usually covers the upper part of the leaves.

To help prevent powdery mildew, water your plants from the base and make sure they get enough sunlight and plenty of air can circulate around them. You can protect plants from powdery mildew by making a spray with 1 part milk and 2–3 parts water and spraying it on your plants every 10–14 days. This works especially well on cucumbers, zucchini, and melons.

If your plants have powdery mildew, you should remove all infected leaves, stems, and fruit and dispose of them. There are a few organic fungicides that work well against powdery mildew, including sulfur, lime-sulfur, neem oil, and potassium bicarbonate. Homemade baking soda fungicide works well too.

Rust

Rust is a common fungal disease spread by wind in wet conditions. Spores land on plants and breed. Plants that can be affected by rust include potatoes, sweet potatoes, carrots, onions, beans, peas, corn, eggplants, okra, artichokes, and asparagus. Plants affected by rust disease will have rust-like spots on their leaves. This strips the nutrients out of plants and stunts their growth. It thrives in the summer when it's warm and humid. If your plants have rust, remove all infected parts and dispose of them. Also, clean away all debris in between plants to prevent rust from spreading. There are a lot of organic

fungicides that can treat rust, so you can ask your local nursery what they have in stock. Neem oil fungicides work well against rust. Homemade baking soda fungicide works well too.

Bacterial Diseases

Plants are typically resistant to bacterial diseases. If your plants are healthy, they shouldn't get bacterial diseases. If pests have attacked plants' leaves or stems, then this could allow bacteria to enter and cause rot in the plants, and the plants may look slimy. There are no treatments for most bacterial diseases, so it is best to get rid of infected plants if this occurs and disinfect gardening tools to stop the bacteria from spreading.

Here is a list of bacterial diseases and their symptoms:

Bacterial Leaf Spot

Bacteria can get into the leaves of your plants and cause spots on the leaves, discoloration, and can cause leaves to die. Bacterial leaf spot spreads in warm and wet conditions. Some of the plants commonly affected by this are lettuce, beets, eggplants, and peppers. You can pick off infected leaves, but if a plant has been systemically infected, you'll need to remove it and dispose of it in the trash. There are no treatments for bacterial leaf spot, but you can use copper fungicides to control the disease in early stages. Baking soda and neem oil fungicides will work too. Remove plant debris, and do not plant new crops where host plants were once growing.[32]

Bacterial Soft Rot

Bacterial soft rots are a group of diseases that cause more crop loss worldwide than any other bacterial disease. Bacterial soft rots affect a wide variety of plants, including a wide range of vegetables, such as lettuce, brassicas (broccoli,

---

[32] Image from: https://www.gardeningknowhow.com/plant-problems/disease/bacterial-leaf-spot.htm

Brussels sprouts, cabbage, cauliflower, collards, kale, mustard, radish), cucurbits (squash, pumpkins, cucumbers, melons), tomatoes, peppers, potatoes, carrots, herbs, and more. Symptoms include wet, slimy, soft rot that affects any part of vegetable crops, including heads, curds, edible roots, stems, and leaves. There is no treatment for bacterial soft rot. If your plants have this, immediately remove and dispose of the infected plants or plant parts.[33]

Black Rot

Black rot is a potentially lethal bacterial disease that affects most brassica crops, such as broccoli, Brussels sprouts, cabbage, cauliflower, collards, kale, mustard, and radish. Symptoms include light-brown or yellow V-shaped lesions on leaves, and the leaves become brittle and dry with age. This disease

thrives in warm and wet conditions. There are no treatments for black rot, but you can use copper fungicides to control the disease in early stages. You can remove infected leaves, but if a plant has been systemically infected, you'll need to remove the whole plant and dispose of it.[34]

Viral Diseases

Viral diseases are spread by insects, and you may notice yellow leaves that twist, crinkle, and then die. There is no treatment for viral diseases, so the best solution is to pull up the infected plants, bag them up, and dispose of them in the trash. Viral diseases are spread by pests, so pest control is key to prevention. Some weeds can be hosts for viral diseases too. While you will rarely get weeds in containers, make sure to remove them if you see any.

---

[33] Image from: https://www.growingproduce.com/vegetables/more-vegetables/take-hard-line-bacterial-soft-rot-pepper/

[34] Image from: https://ag.umass.edu/vegetable/fact-sheets/brassicas-black-rot

Below is a list of viral diseases and their symptoms:

Mosaic Virus

Mosaic viruses are a group of viral diseases that are spread by aphids. There are a lot of different varieties of this virus that affect different plants, for example, cucumber mosaic virus, bean common mosaic virus, potato mosaic virus, and others. It can affect brassicas (broccoli, Brussels sprouts, cabbage, cauliflower, collards, kale, mustard, radish), cucurbits (squash, pumpkins, cucumbers, melons), beans, potatoes, tomatoes, peppers, celery, and other plants. If

your plants have this, their leaves may curl, they won't grow well, and you won't get a bountiful harvest.

There is no treatment for mosaic virus, so you'll need to remove and dispose of any infected plants, including the roots, and also any plants near those affected. Since mosaic viruses are spread by aphids, pest control is key to prevention. Weeds can be hosts for mosaic viruses, so make sure to remove them if you see any. You can also plant virus-resistant plant varieties in your garden.[35]

Tobacco Mosaic Virus

Tobacco mosaic virus is a tobamovirus. Other tobamoviruses include tomato mosaic virus and pepper mild mottle virus. Tobamoviruses are not transmitted by insects. They are highly infectious and very stable in the environment. They can survive on plants, root debris, seeds, tools, and contaminated clothing, which means they can be transmitted by a gardener who has touched

---

[35] Image from: https://www.planetnatural.com/pest-problem-solver/plant-disease/mosaic-virus/

an infected plant. It can affect eggplants, tomatoes, bok choy, bitter melon, long melon, Chinese mustard, snake beans, and Chinese cabbage. Symptoms include leaves having a mosaic pattern on them, mottling, leaf distortion, and sometimes leaves may die and fall off infected plants.

If your plants have this, remove and dispose of them. Burn them if you can, or double bag them and dispose of them in the trash. To help prevent this virus, do not smoke and handle plants or allow tobacco products near the garden. If you notice your plants have this, avoid handling other plants, remove and dispose of infected plants as soon as possible, wash your hands, sanitize your tools, wash your clothes, take a shower, and change your clothes before handling other plants.

Tomato Spotted Wilt Virus

This virus is spread by thrips. It can affect peppers, tomatoes, eggplants, lettuce, celery, peas, potatoes, and sweet basil. Plants infected with this will have bronzing of the upper sides of young leaves, which later develop distinct necrotic spots. Other symptoms include ring spots, line patterns, mottling, and chlorotic blotches on leaves. If your plants have this, remove and dispose of them. Make sure to control thrips and weeds to help prevent it from happening in the future.

Other Diseases

Some diseases can be caused by environmental factors, such as drought, freezing, and other stressors. One of the most common diseases of this type is blossom-end rot.

Blossom-End Rot

Blossom-end rot is an environmental problem, which is typically caused by uneven watering or calcium deficiency. This can mean your tomatoes, peppers, eggplants, or cucumbers have rotten bottoms. Blossom end rot will not spread from plant to plant. To prevent blossom end rot, try to keep your soil evenly moist and add bone meal or oyster shells to your soil to enrich it with calcium.

Disease Prevention

Prevention is better than cure, and that's true with plant health. Below are some things you can do to help prevent diseases in your garden:

1. Water plants at the base and avoid splashing water on leaves or splashing soil on plants. Water plants in the morning to allow any water splashes to dry. This will help prevent fungal diseases.

2. Ensure your plants have sufficient airflow around them and get a good amount of sunlight. If the environment around plants is dark and moist, this is an ideal breeding ground for diseases.

3. Clear any dead leaves, debris, or dead plants because they can house pests and diseases. If you notice any leaves are diseased, remove them and dispose of them in the trash. Do not put them in compost.

4. Wash your hands and tools in between tending to different crops so that you don't spread diseases, like the mosaic virus, unknowingly.

5. If you think you have experienced damping off with seedlings, then get rid of all the soil they were grown in completely, and start again with fresh, soilless seed starting mix.

6. Check any plants you purchase from anywhere for signs of infection before you plant them in your garden.

7. Purchase good quality plants and seeds from reputable suppliers that look healthy (and not spindly).

8. You can also purchase disease-resistant varieties of plants. The seed catalog will generally let you know which varieties are disease resistant. Sometimes when you buy disease-resistant plants, they will have abbreviations such as F2 or F3, which means Fusarium resistance. N stands for nematode resistance. AB means resistant to early blight, and LB means resistant to late blight. PB is resistant to powdery mildew, and

DM resistant to downy mildew. A means anthracnose resistant. S means scab resistant. BMV is bean mosaic virus resistant.

9. Don't put your plants out too early if it's still cold. They won't grow as well and may be more prone to pests and diseases.

10. Mulch larger containers because this will prevent soil from splashing onto the plants. It will also help retain moisture and reduce weeds.

11. Try to prevent pests from damaging your plants because disease-causing organisms can get inside plants through holes and cuts and infect them.

Dealing with Nutrient Deficiencies

As mentioned previously, plants need macronutrients to grow: nitrogen (N), phosphorus (P) and potassium (K). Usually on fertilizer you will see these key figures shown on the side to indicate how much of each of the nutrients is in there.

Nitrogen is essential for photosynthesis and amino acid production. Phosphorus is required for growth and other functions, including photosynthesis and energy transfer. Potassium is used for root growth and photosynthesis.

If plants lack nitrogen, they may be weedy and spindly. Since it is essential for photosynthesis, plants with nitrogen deficiency turn light green in the early stages of growth, and later on they turn yellow because they can't produce chlorophyll, which gives plants their green color.

Phosphorus deficiency can usually be identified at the early vegetative stage of plant growth. Phosphorus deficiency symptoms include reduced shoot growth and increased root growth, which results in a low shoot/root ratio as well as small and dark green leaves.

If your plants are deficient in potassium, you'll see brown scorching and curling of leaf tips as well as chlorosis (yellowing) between leaf veins. Potassium deficiency symptoms first appear on older (lower) leaves because plants can allocate potassium to younger leaves when they are deficient in it. Potassium deficiency is most common in potatoes, beets, brassicas (broccoli,

Brussels sprouts, cabbage, cauliflower, collards, kale, mustard, radish), tomatoes, apples, currants, gooseberries, and raspberries.

Plants also require magnesium for photosynthesis. Some plants need more magnesium than others, such as tomatoes, apples, grapevines, and raspberries. Plants also need calcium, sulfur, manganese, iron, boron, and molybdenum.

Most plants should have their nutrient needs met by a good fertilizer. However, if you notice your plants have signs of nutrient deficiencies, here's what you can do to fix it. If your plants are deficient in nitrogen, you can fertilize them with blood meal or add some compost or manure to the potting soil. Adding compost or manure to containers is simple—just set it around the base of a plant and water it to help the nutrient reach the roots. If you think your plants are deficient in phosphorus, you can fertilize them with bone meal or add rock phosphate to the potting soil. If your plants are deficient in potassium, you can fertilize them with seaweed or kelp fertilizer.

If you are growing tomatoes and the leaves start to turn purple, this can be a sign that the plants do not have enough phosphorus. If you have been using half strength fertilizer, this is a sign that you need to be using full strength fertilizer now. On the fertilizer, the phosphorus content (the middle number) should be a minimum of 3.

When I first started growing tomatoes in containers, we had an infestation of little green aphids that would suck the sap out of the leaves and stems and make the leaves go floppy and yellow. I wanted to use organic solutions to deal with this because we wanted to eat the tomatoes, so using chemical pesticides was a no go. So, in order to get rid of the aphids, we sprayed the plants with a neem oil solution for a couple of weeks, and this did the trick. Our plants could grow healthy and strong.

We also experienced lots of ants around our garden containers once, and this was because the tomatoes and roses in the containers had aphids. The ants protected the aphids because the aphids produced honeydew that was a lovely treat for them. We didn't want the garden swarming with ants, however. So, in order to tackle the ant issue, we soaked the containers in an insecticidal soap solution and also cleared up leaf debris around the containers. Then we sprayed the plants with a neem oil solution to get rid of the aphids. In a couple of weeks, the aphids were gone, and we didn't see the ants anymore.

Key takeaways from this chapter:

1. Check plants for pests twice a week.

2. There are many different types of pests, such as aphids, ants, fungus gnats, leaf miners, mealybugs, nematodes, pill bugs, spider mites, springtails, thrips, and whiteflies.

3. Ants love honeydew created by sap-sucking pests, such as aphids.

4. Neem oil spray works well against a lot of different pests, including aphids, fungus gnats, whiteflies, scales, squash bugs, Colorado potato beetles, and mealybugs.

5. It is a good idea to pick up discarded leaves and bits of plant from around containers to discourage pests and avoid fungus.

6. Wash plants before bringing them into your home over winter to get rid of any diseases.

7. Don't reuse potting soil.

8. If you have been dealing with an infected plant, then wash your hands, tools, and gloves before doing anything with other plants.

9. Dispose of the diseased leaves or fruit, sometimes you may have to remove infected plants and dispose of them.

10. If you dispose of leaves or parts of a plant, place them in a bag in the trash and never put them in compost as this could spread diseases or pests.

11. Water plants at their base so that no water remains settled on the leaves.

12. If you the leaves of your tomato plants turn purple, this can mean that the plant is lacking phosphorus.

The next chapter of the book is my favorite part of having a container garden—harvesting the bounty you have grown in your containers. I can barely think of anything better in life, and I still get excited each time I fill a basket with the lovely produce that I have grown. Eating the produce that you've personally grown and giving some away to friends and family who are always so grateful for it is fabulous. We grow a lot of vegetables, fruits, and herbs, so we make things like chutneys, pickles, jams, soups, pies, smoothies, and much more. We really make the best use of what we grow and try not to waste anything. If we have lots left over, we donate it to a community store or a community kitchen where people on a low income can purchase it for cheap, or we give it away to those who need it. The next chapter will give you tips about how to tell when your plants are ready to harvest and how to store the harvested vegetables and fruits.

Chapter 8: Time to Harvest the Bounty

Personally, I enjoy all stages of the container gardening process. Right from choosing the containers you'll use, the styles, the correct sizes, then working out the best position for them and making your garden both aesthetically pleasing and practical to access, with support for plants that require it. Through to filling the containers with the best potting mix that will help your plants thrive. Then deciding on whether to start your plants from seed or purchase seedlings from a nursery. I enjoy the calming process of maintaining my container garden and how it has naturally become part of my daily routine. It's time for me and my plants, and I find it relaxing and therapeutic. It appeals to all my senses because the plants are beautiful to look at, and they smell incredible. I like the feel of the leaves and soil, and I know the produce is going to taste incredible. But when it comes to harvesting the bounty, I feel this is super rewarding. It feels like it's a way for plants to say thanks for carefully tending to them, watering and feeding them with fertilizer, and you get a chance to eat the beautiful vegetables, fruits, and herbs.

So, this chapter will cover when you should harvest plants and how you can tell they're ready to harvest. It will also cover how you should store your harvest to keep it fresh and preserved.

Harvesting

While seed packets provide information on how long it takes for plants to reach maturity—and this is a helpful guide—there are numerous factors that can change this, including the weather, the quality of your soil, whether your plants got enough water, and so on. But vegetables themselves give some clues as to whether they are mature, and this chapter will help you learn about these.

Some vegetables taste best when they are tender and immature. Things like peas, salad greens, zucchini, cucumbers, beans, potatoes, radishes, cabbage, broccoli, cauliflower, summer squash, and turnips fall into this category. Other plants need to ripen on the vine, such as tomatoes, melons, and winter squash. Most herbs should be harvested before they flower because when they do, herbs lose their flavor.

It is important to regularly check whether your vegetables are ready to be harvested because if you leave some vegetables for too long, they can become tough or overripe. For example, beans can become tough if left for too long, and zucchini can become overripe.

Before you start harvesting, there are certain tools that will come in handy. These include a clean, food-safe container that you can put your produce in—this could be a stainless steel bowl, a plastic bowl, or a basket. You will also need scissors or pruners and food-safe wipes or soap to be able to clean your tools. Ensure that you have washed your hands and tools before starting to harvest to avoid spreading any diseases.

A good time to harvest can be early in the day because it's cool, and your vegetables and fruits will typically be well hydrated. It's best not to harvest when it's raining because water can spread diseases between plants. If you see that any produce has bird or animal droppings on it, do not harvest this because this could spread diseases to you or anyone who eats it. If anything looks like it has been bruised or damaged by animals, I'd avoid harvesting this, but you can place it in the compost bin. If you're harvesting leafy greens, always take the leaves on the outside of plants first because this will allow your plants to keep on growing and thriving.

With other vegetables and fruits that you harvest, ensure that they are ripe and ready to be harvested because then they will be much more flavorsome. Ensure you know what the ripe plant should look like, try to be patient, and resist the urge to pick things too early. The next chapter has more information on when to harvest different vegetables, fruits, and herbs.

For lettuce, kale, and peas, you can pinch off leaves and peas by hand. With lettuce and other leafy vegetables that sprout from the center of the plant, if you're just taking a few leaves and not harvesting the entire thing, then take the outer leaves first so that the plant can continue to grow. If something doesn't come off easily, you can use scissors or a knife. If you have root crops, like potatoes or beets, then you may need to use a fork to harvest them. With herbs and salad leaves, you can use scissors to snip off the leaves, and it's best to take the leaves from around the base of the plant first so that the plant can continue to grow.

Be gentle when you're handling vegetables and fruits so that you don't bruise them. Try to get rid of as much soil and debris as you can from your harvest while still outside so that you don't clog up the sink in your home with soil.

Once you've finished harvesting, ensure everything is cleaned away and keep your produce in the shade before taking it indoors. Clean your harvesting tools. If you're planning on using your harvested produce immediately, then wash it.

Storing Your Harvest

If you're planning on storing your harvested produce away for later use, you can lightly rinse greens and wrap them in a paper towel to store in the fridge. With other vegetables that you harvest, such as tomatoes, peppers, or onions, don't wash these until you need to use them. This will help prevent them from spoiling.

If you want to store vegetables and fruits to eat later, you can store some for months under the right conditions. You need to select vegetables and fruits that are unblemished and check them regularly to make sure any damaged or diseased vegetables or fruits are removed so that they won't spoil the remainder. If you have one rotten piece of fruit or a rotten vegetable, it can ruin all the rest. You can buy wooden crate storage boxes or use shallow cardboard boxes. If you stack these, ensure that there is space between them for air to circulate.

Different vegetables and fruits need different storage conditions. Temperature and humidity are the most important factors to consider. You've probably seen recommendations like "store in a cool, dry place". But exactly does "cool, dry place" mean? There are three combinations for long-term storage:

- Cool and dry (50–60°F (10–15°C) and 60% relative humidity)
- Cold and dry (32–40°F (0–4°C) and 65% relative humidity)
- Cold and moist (32-40°F (0–4°C) and 95% relative humidity)

The ideal temperature for cold conditions is 32°F (0°C). This temperature is not easy to attain in most homes, however. You can expect shortened shelf life for your vegetables the more storage conditions deviate from the ideal temperature. Shelf life shortens approximately 25% for every 10°F (5.5°C) increase in temperature.

Basements are generally cool and dry. If you decide to store vegetables in your basement, they will need some ventilation. Harvested vegetables still "breathe" and need oxygen to maintain their freshness. Also, make sure to protect your stored produce from rodents.

Refrigerators are generally cold and dry. This works well for long-term storage of garlic and onions, but not much else. If you put vegetables in plastic bags in the fridge, this will create too much humidity, which can lead to the growth of mold and bacteria. You can put vegetables in perforated plastic bags, and it will create cold and moist conditions but only for a moderate amount of time.

Root cellars are generally cold and moist. If you store vegetables in a cellar, they'll need some ventilation and protection from rodents. You can use materials such as straw, hay, or wood shavings for insulation. If you decide to use insulation, make sure that it's clean.

You can store apples and pears—a good tip is to wrap each of them in newspaper and place these in just one layer in a container. You can store carrots, potatoes, and beets. To do so, ensure that you have removed the leafy tops off carrots and beets. Don't wrap them, and place them in a single layer. You can cover them with a layer of sand to stop them from going rubbery. You can store potatoes in hessian or paper sacks. It's good to harvest potatoes when the weather is dry and then leave them in the sun to dry. Ensure that mud is removed from potatoes to prevent mold. Ensure potatoes are stored somewhere dark to stop them from going green.

Most vegetables prefer cold and moist conditions, so a root cellar is the perfect place for long-term storage for most vegetables. Storage conditions for different vegetables, fruits, and herbs will be covered below.

Cool and dry conditions are suitable for some pumpkins, zucchini, winter squash, and onions.

Cold and moist conditions are suitable for root crops, such as potatoes, carrots, beets, radishes, turnips, and parsnips, as well as asparagus, beans, broccoli, cabbage, cauliflower, corn, spinach, and peas. Apples and pears can be stored in cold and moist conditions too. Produce that needs cold and moist conditions can be stored in the fridge, but it will last less because refrigerators tend to dry things out.

Some vegetables, such as cucumbers, peppers, tomatoes, and eggplants, require cool and moist storage (55°F or 13°C and 90–95% relative humidity). It's difficult to maintain these conditions in a typical home, so you can expect to keep vegetables that require such storage conditions for only a short period of time.

Berries can't be stored for long. Never rinse berries before storage because it will wash off the thin protective epidermal layer. Place them on a paper towel in a tightly covered container and store them in the fridge for 2–3 days.

If you want to store onions or shallots, these need to be dried, plaited, and stored in a dry place. You can cut the tops off and hang them in tights or netting.

Any leafy vegetables don't store well, and you should ideally eat these within a few days of harvesting them.

Below you will find a table with storage conditions for a variety of different vegetables and fruits as well as their approximate storage life:

Produce	Temperature	Relative humidity (percent)	Approximate storage life
Fruits			
Apples	30–40°F (–1 to +4°C)	90–95	1–12 months
Apricots	31–32°F (–0.5 to 0°C)	90–95	1–3 weeks
Berries			
— Blackberries	31–32°F (–0.5 to 0°C)	90–95	2–3 days
— Elderberries	31–32°F (–0.5 to 0°C)	90–95	1–2 weeks
— Gooseberries	31–32°F (–0.5 to 0°C)	90–95	3–4 weeks

Produce	Temperature	Relative humidity (percent)	Approximate storage life
— Raspberries	31–32°F (–0.5 to 0°C)	90–95	2–3 days
— Strawberries	32°F (0°C)	90–95	3–7 days
— Cherries, sour	32°F (0°C)	90–95	3–7 days
Cherries, sweet	30–31°F (–1 to –0.5°C)	90–95	2–3 weeks
Nectarines	31–32°F (–0.5 to 0°C)	90–95	2–4 weeks
Peaches	31–32°F (–0.5 to 0°C)	90–95	2–4 weeks
Pears	29–31°F (–1.5 to –0.5°C)	90–95	2–7 months
Plums and prunes	31–32°F (–0.5 to 0°C)	90–95	2–5 weeks
Vegetables			
Asparagus	32–35°F (0–1.5°C)	95–100	2–3 weeks
Beans green or snap	40–45°F (4–7°C)	95	7–10 days
Beets, topped	32°F (0°C)	98–100	4–6 months
Broccoli	32°F (0°C)	95–100	10–14 days
Brussels sprouts	32°F (0°C)	95–100	3–5 weeks
Cabbage, early	32°F (0°C)	98–100	3–6 weeks
Cabbage, late	32°F (0°C)	98–100	5–6 months
Carrots	32°F (0°C)	98–100	7–9 months
Cauliflower	32°F (0°C)	95–98	3–4 weeks
Celeriac	32°F (0°C)	97–99	6–8 months
Celery	32°F (0°C)	98–100	2–3 months
Chard	32°F (0°C)	95–100	10–14 days
Corn, sweet	32°F (0°C)	95–98	5–8 days
Cucumbers	50–55°F (10–13°C)	95	10–14 days

Produce	Temperature	Relative humidity (percent)	Approximate storage life
Eggplant	46–54°F (8–12°C)	90–95	1 week
Garlic	32°F (0°C)	65–70	6–7 months
Horseradish	30–32°F (–1 to 0°C)	98–100	10–12 months
Kale	32°F (0°C)	95–100	2–3 weeks
Leeks	32°F (0°C)	95–100	2–3 months
Lettuce	32°F (0°C)	98–100	2–3 weeks
Onions, green	32°F (0°C)	95–100	3–4 weeks
Onions, dry	32°F (0°C)	65–70	1–8 months
Onion sets	32°F (0°C)	65–70	6–8 months
Parsley	32°F (0°C)	95–100	2–2.5 months
Parsnips	32°F (0°C)	98–100	4–6 months
Peas, green	32°F (0°C)	95–98	1–2 weeks
Peppers, chili (dry)	32–50°F (0–10°C)	60–70	6 months
Peppers, sweet	45–55°F (7–13°C)	90–95	2–3 weeks
Potatoes, early crop	40°F (4°C)	90–95	4–5 months
Potatoes, late crop	38–40°F (3–4°C)	90–95	5–10 months
Pumpkins	50–55°F (10–13°C)	50–70	2–3 months
Radishes, spring	32°F (0°C)	95–100	3–4 weeks
Radishes, winter	32°F (0°C)	95–100	2–4 months
Rhubarb	32°F (0°C)	95–100	2–4 weeks
Rutabagas	32°F (0°C)	98–100	4–6 months
Spinach	32°F (0°C)	95–100	10–14 days
Squashes, summer	41–50°F (5–10°C)	95	1–2 weeks
Squashes, winter	50°F (10°C)	50–70	1–6 months

Produce	Temperature	Relative humidity (percent)	Approximate storage life
Sweet potatoes	55–60°F (13–16°C)	85–90	4–7 months
Tomatoes mature, green	55–70°F (13–21°C)	90–95	1–3 weeks
Tomatoes firm, ripe	55–70°F (13–21°C)	90–95	4–7 days
Turnips	32°F (0°C)	95	4–5 months

Storing your harvest is not the only way to preserve it, of course. You can preserve your harvest with pickling, canning, making jams, freezing, and drying, and I could write a book about it. In fact, I did, and I'd like you to have it for free as a way of saying thanks for purchasing this book. To get your free eBook, please scan the QR code on page 4 or send me an email to maxbarnesbooks@gmail.com and I will send you the free eBook.

I will never forget when we first harvested produce from our container garden. We had an abundance of tomatoes of all shapes and sizes, from cherry tomatoes to large Marmande Superprecoce tomatoes. We had cucumbers, peppers, chilis, green beans, peas, lots of beautiful smelling basil (it's my favorite herb, and I adore the smell), eggplants, and strawberries. The first meal that included our fresh produce was incredible. We sat and ate it outside on the table on the patio, and it was wonderful to ladle food onto your plate that was made from the produce you've personally grown. We stayed out until the sunset and had a lovely time. The food could not be any fresher! It tasted delicious, and every flavor seemed enhanced. For nights after that, we became inventive with tomato and chili soups, passata for pizzas or pastas, and we had lovely lasagnas containing all our homegrown ingredients.

Key takeaways from this chapter:

1. Ensure you have food-safe containers to gather your harvest and store it in. You will also need scissors or pruners and wipes for hands and tools. This will help your harvesting to go smoothly.

2. Harvest vegetables and fruits early in the day when the weather is dry.

3. Never harvest any vegetables or fruits that have bird or animal droppings on them or those that are damaged or bruised. Compost them instead.

4. With leafy vegetables, always take the outside leaves first when harvesting.

5. Harvest vegetables and fruits when they are ripe, mature, soft to touch, and not hard. Always be gentle when harvesting.

6. If you are planning to eat them soon, rinse greens and put them in the fridge. With other vegetables, don't wash them until you need to use them.

7. To keep vegetables and fruits stored for longer, choose healthy and unblemished vegetables and fruits. Check your stored vegetables and fruits regularly to make sure none are rotten because this can affect the rest of the stored produce and ruin it.

8. Store vegetables and fruits in one layer in crates or boxes. Wrap apples and pears in paper. Don't wrap carrots, potatoes, and beets.

9. Cut the leafy tops off carrots and beets. Cover them in sand to prevent them from going rubbery.

10. Harvest potatoes when it's dry, and allow them to dry in the sun. Make sure there is no mud on them because this can cause them to go moldy.

11. Use leafy vegetables within a few days.

The next chapter will look at plant profiles of different vegetables and fruits. This will help you when selecting the best type of plants to grow in your container garden. The chapter will give you information on what size containers different plants need, how big they will grow, their sun requirements, what conditions they prefer, how much water and fertilization they need, and when they should be harvested. This chapter will help you make better choices before selecting plants to grow. It will cover a variety of vegetables, fruits, herbs, and flowers that grow well in containers.

Chapter 9: Plant Profiles

This chapter is here to help you make informed decisions about what plants you could grow in your container garden. By knowing in advance how big plants will grow, you can place the seeds or seedlings into appropriately sized containers. You will know sun requirements of different plants, and therefore where you'll need to position them in your garden. You will also know how much water plants need and how to fertilize them to keep them in optimum health. You'll also know how much care plants will likely need throughout their lifetime.

All plants can be classified as annuals, biennials, or perennials—these terms are related to the life cycle of plants. Annuals complete their entire life cycle in just one year. They go from seed to plant to flower to seed again during that one year. Only the seed survives to start the next generation, and the rest of the plant dies. Biennials take up to two years to complete their life cycle. They produce vegetation in the first year. In the second year, they produce flowers and seeds that go on to produce the next generation. Many vegetables are biennials but are often grown as annuals. Perennials live more than two years—from three years to hundreds of years. The above-ground portion of the plant may die in the winter and come back from the roots the following year. Some plants may retain foliage throughout the winter. Trees and shrubs are perennials.

This chapter covers 25 vegetables, 10 fruits, 10 herbs, and 5 flowers. Clearly, this chapter won't cover every type of plant you may wish to grow in your containers, but for a beginner just starting out, it will give you some good pointers as to some of the more common plants people grow in containers and what to expect from them.

Vegetables

Beets (Beetroot)

Ideally, you'll need a container that's 10–12 inches (25–30 cm) deep to grow beets; however, an 8-inch (20 cm) container is doable. Width is not as important as depth. The wider your container is, the more beets you can grow. You can grow 5–6 beets in a 2-gallon (7.8L) container.

Beets don't like to be transplanted, so you'll need to start them directly in containers you'll grow them in. You can sow the seeds 3 weeks before the last frost. They need to be spaced 3 inches from one another.

Beets can be grown in full or partial sun, and they will need at least 6 hours of sunlight per day. Beets are biennial plants grown as annuals. They are a cool-season crop, and they grow best in temperatures between 50 and 85°F (10–30°C). You need to water them regularly so that the soil is moist at all times. Do not let it dry out completely. It's a good idea to use either time-based (slow-release) fertilizer or compost to enrich the soil when they sprout, and then fertilize them again with a balanced liquid fertilizer around 5 weeks after that when they break the soil surface. Beets are a root vegetable, so they need a fertilizer that is low in nitrogen but high in phosphorus and potassium.

Beets typically take 6–9 weeks to get ready for harvest after germination. You can also harvest beet greens to use in salads—their tender leaves taste delicious. You can start harvesting greens when leaves are a few inches long by cutting the outer leaves only and leaving the small inner foliage to grow, which you can harvest later.

Broccoli

Broccoli need a 12-inch (30 cm) deep container at a minimum. Ideally, they need a container that is 12–18 (30–45cm) inches deep. Growing one plant in a single container is usually best; however, you can grow multiple plants in large containers. For example, you can grow 2–3 plants in a container that is 18 inches (45 cm) wide.

You can start broccoli from seed. Sow the seeds ½ inch (0.6 cm) deep in individual pots filled with seed starting mix. Give them plenty of light and water them regularly. They will germinate in 1–2 weeks. Once they are 3–7 inches (7.5–18 cm) tall and have 4 true leaves, you can transplant them into growing pots.

Broccoli need full sun and at least 6 hours of sunlight per day. They are a cool-season crop, and they do best in temperatures below 75°F (24°C). Broccoli are biennial plants grown as annuals. They can grow 18–30 inches (45–75 cm) tall and up to 18 inches (45 cm) wide. They like soil to be moist, so make sure to water them regularly. Ensure the containers have good drainage because overwatering can cause root rot. Broccoli love cool soil, so mulching is a good idea. You can add a 2-inch (5cm) layer of mulch when planting. It will help keep the soil cool and will help keep the moisture in. You can add compost to the soil when planting and then once again in mid-season. Alternatively, you can use a slow-release balanced fertilizer at the time of planting and then add a balanced liquid fertilizer every two weeks. You may need to prune them if you notice vigorous growth. You'll need to pinch out newly developing side shoots, and you can also cut away wilting leaves from sides. But don't go too hard on it and avoid excessive pruning.

Broccoli will be ready to harvest in 60–80 days after transplanting into growing containers. Look out for light green buds, and cut them with 4–5 inches (10–12.5 cm) of stem, but leave the outer leaves intact because they are going to encourage new growth.

Cabbage

Cabbage can be grown in containers. Your containers need to be at least 12 inches (30 cm) deep and 18 inches (45 cm) wide.

Cabbage can be started indoors early for fall and spring crops or purchased as transplants for a fall crop. You can start cabbage indoors 6–8 weeks before transplanting. Plant the seeds ¼ to ½ inch (0.6–1.2 cm) deep. You can transplant your cabbage seedlings 1–2 weeks before the last frost after they've been hardened off outside for a week for spring harvest, or you can direct sow cabbage 6–8 weeks before the first frost in the fall for fall harvest.

Cabbage needs full sun with 6–8 hours of sunlight per day. Cabbage is a cool-season crop, and it grows best when the temperature is between 60 and 65°F (15–18°C) and no higher than 75°F (24°C). Cabbage is a biennial plant grown as an annual. Cabbage needs frequent watering. Water it when the top 2 inches (5 cm) of soil are dry. You can fertilize cabbage with a balanced liquid fertilizer every 2–3 weeks. Compost tea works great for cabbage.

Cabbage generally takes around 70–80 days to reach maturity; however, some varieties can take up to 4–6 months to grow, depending on the type. Harvest them once they have reached the size you want and formed a firm head. To harvest, cut each cabbage head at the base with a sharp knife, remove any yellow leaves, but keep loose green leaves because they provide protection in storage, and immediately bring the head indoors or place it in shade.

Carrots

The container that you put them in needs to be at least 8 inches (20 cm) deep for short or half-long varieties and 12 inches (30 cm) deep for standard length carrots. If you decide to grow really large carrots, like Imperator carrots, you'll need a container that's 16–18 inches (40–45 cm) deep because these carrots can grow up to 12 inches (30 cm) long.

Carrots don't like to be transplanted, so plant them directly in the containers you intend to grow them in. You can sow seeds 2–3 weeks before the last frost. Carrot seeds should be placed 1/4–1/2 inch (0.6–1.2 cm) below the surface of the soil. Spread out the seeds about ½ inch apart. When they grow, they need 3 inches (7.5 cm) of space between them, so you may need to pinch some seeds out.

Carrots like full sun. They need at least 6 hours of sunlight per day. They are biennial plants grown as annuals. Carrots are a cool-season crop, and the ideal temperature for them is 60–72°F (15–22°C). If you live in a warm area, you may grow them in the fall and even in the winter. The soil around them needs to be fluffy and not compacted. Just like with most cool-season crops, mulching the soil is a good idea. Add a 2-inch (5cm) layer of mulch when planting—it will help keep the soil cool and will help keep the moisture in. When the carrot tops appear, fertilize them with a liquid fertilizer every 3–4 weeks. Carrots are a root crop, so a low-nitrogen fertilizer usually works well. They will need to be watered often and their soil should be kept moist. If the soil dries out, the roots may crack, and you will get a poor harvest. They will bloom in the spring.

You can usually harvest carrots 60–75 days after sowing. Pull one up and see how it is when you think the time is right.

Cauliflower

For cauliflower, you'll need a container that's 12 inches (30 cm) deep and 10–12 inches (25–30 cm) wide. You can grow one plant in a pot this size, and it's best to grow cauliflower plants in individual pots. However, you can grow 2–3 plants in large pots, barrels, or grow bags.

You can start cauliflower seeds indoors about a month before the last frost. Sow the seeds in seed starting mix ½ inch (1.2 cm) deep and 1 ½ inches (4 cm) apart. Once the seedlings have germinated and have 3 or 4 true leaves, you can transplant them into growing containers.

Cauliflower grows best in full sun, and it needs 6–8 hours of sunlight per day. It's a cool-season crop, and it does best in moderate temperatures (60–75°F or 15–24°C). Cauliflowers are biennial plants grown as annuals. They can grow 12–30 inches (30–75 cm) tall and 12–30 inches (30–76 cm) wide depending on the variety. Cauliflower grows best in moist soil, so you'll need a growing medium that holds moisture but also drains well. You can add 1/4 part peat moss or coco peat to your potting mix to help with that. Mulching is not necessary when growing cauliflowers, but you can do it to help keep the soil cool and keep the moisture in. Cauliflowers need to be fertilized a lot. You can add compost or well-rotted manure to the soil when you plant them. You'll need to add compost in mid-season as well. Alternatively, you can use a balanced liquid fertilizer once a month or according to the product's instructions.

Cauliflowers are typically ready to harvest 3–4 months after planting. Cauliflower is ready to be harvested when the head is fully developed. It should be 6–12 inches (15–30 cm) in diameter and still compact.

Celery

You'll need a container that's at least 8 inches (20 cm) deep to grow celery. You can grow several plants in one container if it's wide enough—they need to be spaced 10 inches (25 cm) apart.

You will need to start celery from seed indoors and transplant it outside into containers when it is ready. You can sow the seeds 8–12 weeks before the last frost. It's a good idea to soak celery seeds in water overnight before sowing. The seeds are small but should ideally be sown about an inch (2.5 cm) apart. When the seedlings are 2 inches (5 cm) tall, transplant them into individual pots. Introduce them to the outdoors gradually because they don't like cold weather. Seedlings should be put into containers outside 8 to 10 inches (20–25 cm) apart. They do need a lot of water to prevent the celery from becoming stringy and tough. When the seedlings are at least 6 inches (15 cm) tall, you can put mulch around them to keep the soil cool and keep the moisture in. Celery needs compost enriched soil and some fertilizer too. The soil should retain moisture but still drain.

Celery grows best in full sun, but it can grow in partial sun too. It needs 5–7 hours of sunlight per day. Celery is a cool-season crop that prefers temperatures between 65 and 70°F (15–21°C). Celery is a biennial plant grown as an annual. They can grow 18–24 inches (45–60 cm) tall. Celery loves water, so you'll need to keep the soil moist. As mentioned previously, celery needs nutrient-rich soil. You can add compost at the time of planting, and then you'll need to fertilize it with a low-nitrogen liquid fertilizer every month.

When celery starts to grow, you can tie the stalks together to keep them together and stop them from sprawling. You can harvest whole plants or just a stalk or two as you need them to keep the plants growing longer. The darker the stalks are, the more nutrients they contain, but darker green stalks are tougher. You can store celery in the fridge in a plastic bag for a few weeks.

When it's ready, the stalks will typically be around 12–18 inches (30–45 cm). It usually takes 130–140 days to grow before harvesting. Harvest stalks from the outside in. You can harvest the plants whole, but cutting individual stalks will keep plants producing for a longer period of time.

Collard Greens

Collard greens grow big, so if you want to grow them in containers, you'll need big ones that are at least 3 gallons in volume (14.4L), but 5-gallon (19L) containers would be ideal.

You can start collard greens indoors 4–6 weeks before the last frost and transplant them to containers outside 1–2 weeks after the last frost for spring harvest. Or you can start them 3 months before the first frost and transplant them to containers outside 2 months before the first frost for fall harvest. Plant the seeds ¼ to ½ inch (0.6–1.2 cm) deep.

Collard greens prefer growing in full sun, but they will tolerate some shade as long as they get at least 5 hours of sunlight per day. They are a cool-season crop, and they prefer cooler temperature between 55 and 75°F (13–24°C). Collard greens are a biennial crop grown as an annual. They are quite thirsty and need frequent watering. Water them when the top 2 inches (5 cm) of soil are dry. Collard greens don't need a lot of fertilizing—you can fertilize them every 4–6 weeks with a high-nitrogen liquid fertilizer, although a balanced liquid fertilizer would work fine too.

Collard greens usually take 80 days to grow from seed to harvest. You can harvest the leaves as needed or harvest whole plants. Collard leaves are ready for harvest as soon as they reach usable size. You can pick a couple of outer leaves at a time—use scissors or a sharp kitchen knife to cut the leaves about an inch (2.5 cm) from where they jut out of the soil. They will be most tasty when picked young—less than 10 inches (25 cm) long and dark green. If you want to harvest the whole plant, you can cut it off above the crown if there's still some time for it to produce a few more leaves before the growing season ends. Or if the growing season is ending soon, you can pull the whole plant up and cut the roots off once it's out of the ground.

Corn

Corn can be grown in containers. You can choose dwarf varieties that won't exceed 4–5 feet (1.2-1.5 m) in height to grow in containers. You'll need a container that is at least 12 inches (30 cm) wide and deep to grow corn. Each container of this size can hold 4 corn plants.

Corn does not transplant well, so it's best to start it directly in the containers you'll grow it in 1 week before the last frost. You can move the containers outside 2–3 weeks after the last frost.

Corn grows best in full sun with at least 8 hours of sunlight per day, but 10 hours is ideal. It's a warm-season crop, and it grows best in temperatures between 85 and 95°F (30–35°C). Corn is an annual. You would typically need to water corn every other day, but if the weather is really hot, you'll need to water it daily. Corn needs to be fertilized once the plants are 4 weeks old and then again when the plants are 8–10 weeks old with a balanced liquid fertilizer. Corn plants are sturdy and shouldn't need support.

Corn usually takes 90–120 days to grow from seed to harvest, depending on the variety and the weather. Corn is ready for harvest about 20 days after the silk first appears. Corn silk is the long, thread-like strands of plant material that grow underneath the husk of a fresh ear of corn. At harvest time, the silk turns brown, but the husks are still green. When you go to harvest corn, simply take your ear of corn, and bend it downwards and away from the stalk, and it should snap right off. Be careful not to damage the stalk because there might be a few more ears ready to pick in a week or so.

Cucamelons

You'll need at least a 5-gallon (19L) container to grow cucamelons, and you can grow 1 plant in a container this size. You can grow 3–4 plants in large 20–25-gallon (76–95L) containers.

Cucamelons are wonderful in salads, with a taste that is between a cucumber and a lime. They tend to grow to 1–1 5/8 inches (2.5–4 cm) in length. You can start cucamelons from seed indoors, and they should germinate in 10 days. The seeds should be sown 3/8 inch (1 cm) deep with the blunt end downwards. When the seedlings have grown, put them into individual 4-inch pots to grow further. When the frost has passed, you can transfer them into containers outdoors. They should be 1–1.3 feet (30–40 cm) apart, and they'll need canes to support them.

Cucamelons grow best in full sun. They need 6–8 hours of sunlight per day. They are a warm-season crop, and they grow best in temperatures between 65 and 75°F (18–24°C). Cucamelon is a perennial crop in tropical climates, but it's most commonly grown as an annual in other climates, where it is planted in the spring. You'll need to water them regularly and feed them with liquid tomato fertilizer. They can grow up to 1 feet (30 cm) tall and 7–10 feet (2.1–3 m) wide, so they'll need a stable support to thrive, such as a trellis. If the main shoot reaches 8 feet (2.4 m), you can pinch out the growing tip, and you can pinch out the side shoots when they've grown to 16 inches (40 cm).

They will fruit between July and September. When they are the size of olives or grapes, they are ready to eat. Cucamelons usually take 60–70 days to grow after transplanting. Fruits start to appear 2–3 weeks after flowering. Pick them when they're nice and firm. If you leave them on the plant for too long, then they can become bitter and soggy.

Cucumbers

To grow cucumbers in containers, you will need a large pot that ideally holds 5 gallons (19L) of soil or more and is at least 8 inches (20 cm) deep. The container needs to be 10–12 inches (25–30 cm) wide. You can grow 2–3 plants in a 10-inch (25 cm) container and 4–6 plants in a 20-inch (50 cm) container.

You can sow cucumber seeds indoors 2–3 weeks before the last frost, ideally with a heating pad under them to encourage growth. Seeds should be planted 1 inch (2.5 cm) deep. Place the cucumber plants outside 2 weeks after the last frost. Cucumbers don't like frost or cold, so don't plant them out too soon. You can plant every 2 weeks if you'd like a succession of cucumbers.

Cucumbers like to grow in full sun and need 6–8 hours of sunlight per day. They are a warm-season crop that grows best in temperatures between 75 and 85°F (24–30°C). Cucumbers are annual plants. They love sun and water, so you'll need to water them constantly and keep them warm. They do best in soil that has compost in it, and you'll need to fertilize them with a low-nitrogen liquid fertilizer every 3 weeks. You can mulch the soil after planting. The main thing cucumbers need to grow well is lots of water. If you think of how much of the inside of a cucumber is water, it's no wonder that they need to be watered regularly. Don't grow cucumbers too large because they can start to taste bitter. Cucumbers can grow on a vine or on a bush. Vines tend to be more common—they have large leaves and will produce an abundant crop. You will need to have a trellis or a fence to support them. Vine varieties can grow 6–8 feet (1.8–2.4 m) tall and bush varieties can grow 24–36 inches (60–90 cm) tall and wide.

Cucumbers typically take 55–70 days to grow from germination to harvesting. Cucumbers are ready to harvest when they are bright, medium to dark green, and firm. You should avoid harvesting them when they are yellow, puffy, have sunken areas, or wrinkled tips.

Eggplants

You'll need a container that is at least 12 inches (30 cm) deep for eggplants. It's best to grow them in individual containers.

You can start eggplants from seed. You can sow the seeds 4–6 weeks before the last frost. You can plant up to two seeds in each cell of a seed starting tray or sow two seeds in each container directly. Eggplants love warmth even more than tomatoes and peppers. Seedlings will be ready to transplant in about 6–8 weeks. When they have up to four leaves, they can be transplanted into growing containers.

Eggplants grow best in full sun and need 6–8 hours of sunlight per day. They are a warm-season crop that grows best in temperatures between 70 and 85°F (21–30°C). They are biennial plants grown as annuals. Eggplant plants can grow between 2 and 4 feet (0.6–1.2 m) tall and wide. Eggplants love to grow in evenly moist soil, so you'll need to water them regularly, but avoid overwatering them so as not to cause root rot. Eggplants need a fertilizer that is high in phosphorus, but you can use a balanced fertilizer too. Growing eggplants is similar to growing tomatoes. You don't need to prune eggplants, but doing so will help improve the productivity of your plants. You'll need to remove suckers when the plants are mature. You can also remove yellowing or diseased leaves and branches growing tall and lanky. Eggplant bush can grow quite tall, so you'll need to tie your plants to a stake.

Eggplants usually take 2–3 months to grow to harvest after transplanting. Harvest eggplants with skin that is glossy and thin.

Garlic

You'll need a container that's 8 inches (20 cm) deep for garlic. You can plant 3 cloves in a 6-inch (15 cm) pot, 6 cloves in an 8-inch (20 cm) pot, and 8–10 cloves in a 12-inch (25 cm) pot.

Garlic is grown from cloves. Gently separate the cloves and plant them at a depth of 1 inch (2.5 cm) fat end downwards, pointy end up directly in the desired containers. You would typically plant garlic in March, but it depends on the climate you live in. You should ensure they are spaced 4–6 inches (10–15 cm) apart.

Garlic grows best in full sun, and it needs 6–8 hours of sunlight per day. It's a perennial crop grown as an annual. Garlic is a cool-season crop, and it requires cool air temperatures of 32 to 50°F (0–10°C) during its first two months of growth when roots are established and bulbs begin to form. Garlic plants can grow 18–24 inches (45–60 cm) tall. You need to water garlic only 2–3 times a week. You can fertilize garlic in early spring with a fertilizer high in nitrogen—blood meal is perfect for garlic. You can fertilize it again when bulbs begin to form, usually in early May.

If you plant garlic in March, you'll need to water your garlic throughout April to June, and you should be able to harvest it garlic in July or August. It's easy to grow, and it has a long growing season. If you have purchased a hardneck (rather than softneck) variety, this will produce a flower which you should remove when it appears so that the energy can go into growing the bulb instead. If you intend to store garlic, leave it to dry for a few days in the sun before storing.

Green Beans

You can grow beans in containers. The container needs to be at least 6–7 inches (15–18 cm) deep for bush beans and 8–9 inches (20–23 cm) deep for pole beans. If you want to grow several bean plants in one container, it should be wide enough so that the plants don't touch each other. The container should have plenty of drainage holes because beans don't do well if they're stood in water. If you want to make use of vertical space, then pole beans are a good option. They can grow up fences, stakes, and other support systems. Pole beans will take longer before you're able to harvest them, though. You can also get bush beans which tend to grow 18–24 inches (45–60 cm) in height, and you can usually harvest these within 2 months.

Green beans don't like being transplanted, so it's best to start them in containers directly. Sow the seeds just after the last frost. It is best to plant beans in the spring, and they will start to flower 8 weeks later. Bush green beans will grow 2 feet (60 cm) tall and wide, while pole beans can grow anywhere between 6 and 15 feet tall (1.8–5 m) and generally 2–3 feet (60–90 cm) wide.

Green beans require full sun. They need 6–8 hours of sunlight per day. Green beans are a warm-season crop that grows best when temperatures range from 65 to 85°F (18–30°C). They are annual plants. Ensure that there isn't too much shade where you plant them. Pole beans will need a support that is 6–8 feet (1.8–2.4 m) tall, and it's best to have the support in place before planting. Supports should be placed 3–4 feet (0.9–1.2 m) apart. Beans need to be watered regularly. Avoid getting water on the leaves if possible. They don't need to be fertilized much. Beans enrich the soil with nitrogen themselves, so you can fertilize them with a low-nitrogen liquid fertilizer once a month during the growing season. You can also add some compost halfway through growing.

When beans are the size of a small pencil, they can be harvested, which is typically 50–55 days after planting. They are ready to harvest when the pods are 4–6 inches (10–15 cm) long and slightly firm and before the beans protrude through the skin.

Kale

Kale is a leafy green plant which contains lots of vitamins and nutrients. It grows quickly, and just 3–4 plants would be enough for a family of four each week. The ideal container to grow kale would be 12 inches (30 cm) wide and 8 inches (20 cm) deep. It needs to have plenty of drainage, and the potting mix should be nutrient dense too.

You can grow kale in the spring or fall. If you want to grow it in the spring, you can start it indoors 4–6 weeks before the last frost and move the containers outside 1–2 weeks before the last frost. And if you want to grow it in the fall, you should start it 3 months before the first frost. Seeds should be planted ½ inch (1.2 cm) deep and 1 inch (2.5 cm) apart. Generally, seedlings will appear in 2 weeks.

Kale is a vegetable that likes to be grown in full or partial sun. It needs at least 6 hours of sunlight per day, but it grows best in full sun with 6–8 hours of sunlight per day. Kale is a cool-season crop that grows best in temperatures between 65 and 75°F (18–24°C). Kale is a biennial plant grown as an annual. They can grow 1–2 feet (30–60 cm) tall and wide. You should add compost to the soil before planting. You can also consider adding blood meal or cottonseed meal to the soil. You can mulch the top of the soil to help keep the soil cool and keep the moisture in. Kale needs to be watered regularly. You can fertilize kale once a month. Fish emulsion works great for kale in my experience.

Kale usually takes about 3 months to grow from seed to harvest. When kale leaves are approximately the size of your hand, they're ready to be harvested. Harvest lower outer leaves, leaving inner leaves to grow. You can harvest a good fistful of leaves each time you harvest, but don't take more than one third of a plant at a time. If any leaves are yellow, compost them.

Leeks

If you want to grow leeks in containers, you'll need a container that's 10 inches (25 cm) wide and 2–3 gallons (7.6–11.4L) in volume. You can grow 5 leeks in a container this size.

Leeks are best started indoors. You can start leeks indoors 10–12 weeks before the last frost and transplant them outside a week after the last frost. Sow the seeds ¼ to ½ inch (0.6–1.2 cm) deep. When you go to transplant them, plant them 6 inches (15 cm) apart with 12–16 inches (30–40 cm) of space between rows.

Leeks grow best in full sun with 6–8 hours of sunlight per day. Leeks are a cool-season, and they grow best in temperatures between 55 and 75°F (13–24°C). Leeks are technically perennials, although many gardeners treat them as annuals. Leeks need to be watered regularly. They also need a lot of nitrogen. You can fertilize them with fish emulsion or any other nitrogen-rich fertilizer about 3 weeks after planting, and then continue to fertilize every 3–4 weeks during the growing season.

Leeks have a long growing season and take 120–150 days to grow to maturity. Leeks are ready for harvest when their white stem or shaft is 3 inches (7.5 cm) long. You should harvest leeks before they start to widen too much at the base. Also, don't allow leeks to form bulbs. You can harvest leeks from loose soil by gently twisting and pulling them up. Leeks have large root systems, so you can use a hand fork or garden fork to loosen the soil before lifting leeks.

Lettuce

Lettuce is very easy to grow in containers, and the containers don't have to be too deep— 6 inches (15 cm) deep is sufficient. You can grow lettuce leaf, which means you can grow this closer together than a whole head of lettuce—you can put them approximately 4 inches (10 cm) apart.

You can start lettuce seeds indoors 2–4 weeks before the last frost in a seed starting tray or directly in the containers that you intend to grow them in. Lettuce grows fast, so you can stagger how often you plant new seeds according to how quickly you harvest it. Introduce lettuce seedlings to the outdoors gradually, increasing their time spent outdoors over a week. Lettuce seeds are small and should be planted ¼ inch (6 mm) deep. They will require light to germinate, so don't plant them too deep. Depending on what type of lettuce you have planted will determine what space you'll need between your seedlings once they start to grow. You'll need to thin them out accordingly. Loose leaf lettuce needs to be 4 inches (10 cm) apart. Romaine lettuce should be 8 inches (20 cm) apart. Iceberg lettuce needs to be 16 inches (40 cm) apart. Your rows of lettuce themselves should be 16 inches (40 cm) apart.

Lettuce needs full or partial sun to grow and at least 5–6 hours of sunlight per day. It grows best in full sun with 8 hours of sunlight per day, though. Lettuce is a cool-season crop that prefers temperatures between 60 and 70°F (15–21°C). Lettuce is an annual plant. Lettuce plants can grow 6–12 inches (15–30 cm) tall and 2–12 inches (5–30 cm) wide. Lettuce can keep growing for quite some time—the key requirement is that it gets plenty of water. If the weather is really hot, then lettuce may want some shade in the afternoon. You can add some compost to the soil too. You can cover the soil around lettuce with mulch. You will need to keep the soil really moist when you grow lettuce. Keep in mind that containers dry out much quicker than soil in the garden does. The soil in containers should be moist but not soggy. If the leaves look like they're wilting, water them. Lettuce needs plenty of fertilizer to help it keep producing new leaves, so make sure to feed it every two weeks with a balanced liquid fertilizer. A top tip is that you could consider growing chives or garlic in between your lettuce rows because this would prevent aphids.

Lettuce grows fairly quickly. Leaf varieties reach maturity in 30 days, but they can be harvested as soon as they reach the desired size. Other types of lettuce require 6 to 8 weeks to reach full harvest size. It's best to harvest lettuce in the morning and take young and tender leaves. Always take the outer leaves and let the inner leaves grow.

Onions

You need a container that's 10 inches (25 cm) deep for onions. It also needs to be as wide as possible to make it worth your while. They need at least 3 inches (7.5 cm) of soil around them to grow properly.

You can grow onions from seed or sets. Sets are essentially baby onions. Growing from sets is easier and quicker than growing from seed; however, growing from seed is not difficult. Growing from seed also allows for more choice of variety. You can sow seeds 4–6 weeks before the last frost. Plant them about ½ inch deep (1.2 cm) and water them regularly. They will be ready for transplanting in about 12 weeks. Onions need 1.5–2 inches (4–5 cm) of spacing when you plant them. If you decide to grow from sets, simply plant them directly in your chosen container.

Onions need full sun. Onions begin to form bulbs when a certain day length is reached. Short-day onion varieties begin to form bulbs when they receive 11 or 12 hours of daylight, intermediate-day onions need 12 to 14 hours of daylight, and long-day varieties require 14 or more hours of daylight. Onions are a cool-season crop that grows best in temperatures between 55 and 75°F (13–24°C). They are biennial plants grown as annuals. Onion plants can grow 10–30 inches (25–75 cm) tall, 4–24 inches (10–60 cm) wide, and produce bulbs that are 1–6 inches (2.5–15 cm) in diameter. They need to be watered regularly. You'll need to fertilize your onions with a liquid fertilizer that's high in nitrogen every 2–3 weeks.

Onions need 90–100 days to grow from seed to harvest. You'll know they're ready to harvest when the leaves droop and turn yellow or brown. Gently loosen the soil around them and then lift the onions out to harvest them. All varieties of onions will grow green stalks, and you can harvest them 3–4 weeks after planting once they're 6–8 inches (15–20 cm). Simply cut the largest outer ones, leaving at least an inch (2.5 cm) above the soil. Harvest about a third of the stalks each time.

Peas

Peas grow well in containers, and you can grow dwarf or bush varieties of peas. You can also use a trellis or a support system for the peas to grow up. You don't need to have a massive container, and it's more important for the container to be wide rather than deep. An 8–12-inch (20–30 cm) deep container is fine, and it should be as wide as possible. For tall and large bushier varieties, choose pots that are 8–12 inches (20–30 cm) deep and as wide as possible. You can grow multiple plants in one container. The plants need to be spaced 3 to 5 inches (7.5–12.5 cm).

Growing peas from seed is not difficult at all. Sow the seeds 4–6 weeks before the last frost 1–2 inches (2.5–5 cm) apart either in a seed starting tray or directly in containers. Seeds will germinate in 7–30 days, and you can transplant them into containers outside when they are 4–5 inches (10–12.5 cm) tall. You can soak seeds in water for 24 hours before planting to speed up the germination process.

Peas can grow in partial sun, but they grow best in full sun. They need 6–8 hours of sunlight per day. Peas are a cool-season crop that grows best in temperatures between 55 and 65°F (15–18°C). They don't like temperatures over 70°F (21°C). Peas are annual plants. Peas prefer growing in cool and moist soil, but don't overwater it so that it doesn't become soggy. Mulching is not really necessary, but it can help keep the soil cool if you live in a hotter climate. Peas don't need a lot of fertilizing. Feeding them with a balanced liquid fertilizer every 2–3 weeks is enough. Peas are natural climbers, and they need support to grow in most cases. Bushier or dwarf varieties can do without support, but they won't produce a bountiful crop. Vining peas definitely need a trellis—they can grow up to 8 feet (2.4 m) tall. Bush peas can grow 18–30 (45–75 cm) tall and can also benefit from support, especially when they grow over 2 feet (60 cm) tall.

Most varieties of peas need 60–70 days to grow from planting to harvest. Harvest pea pods when they are bright green and noticeably full. They should be plump and swollen.

Peppers

You can grow any variety of peppers in containers, including bell preppers and chili peppers, and their requirements are quite similar. The correct pot to grow peppers needs to be at least 12 inches (30 cm) deep. The container should have good drainage and needs frequent watering.

You can start peppers from seed, and you should sow them 6–10 weeks before the last frost. For bell peppers, plant the seeds about an inch (2.5 cm) deep, and for chili peppers, about a ¼ of an inch (0.6 cm) deep. Seeds will germinate in 1–3 weeks. When they have at least 2 true leaves, they can be transplanted into the desired containers. You can move them outside 2 weeks after the last frost.

Peppers require full sun, and they need at least 6–8 hours of sunlight per day, but they will grow best with up to 12 hours of sunlight per day. Peppers are a warm-season crop that grows best in temperatures between 70 and 80°F (21–27°C). Peppers are perennial plants grown as annuals. They can grow 3–6 feet (0.9–1.8 m) tall and 18–24 inches (45–60 cm) wide. Peppers need to be watered regularly, so keep the soil slightly moist and don't let it dry out completely. Try to avoid getting the leaves wet because this can cause fungal infections. Mulching the soil is a good idea when growing peppers, as it will help keep the soil cool and keep the moisture in. Peppers need to be fertilized regularly, just like tomatoes. A fertilizer with a lower nitrogen number is perfect, but a balanced fertilizer works well too, and you should use it every 2 weeks. Pepper plants can benefit from having support—stakes and cages are popular options for that. You can pinch pepper plants when they are at least 6 inches (15 cm) tall—simply clip the growing tip. You can also deadhead the flowers if they start appearing too early—this will help direct the plant's energy into growth.

Bell peppers take 2–3 months to be ready for harvesting after transplanting, and chili peppers can take 2–4 months to grow. You can harvest bell peppers when they're green once they reach full size and remain firm. Or you can leave them to ripen, and their color will change into red, yellow, or orange. As for chili peppers, you can harvest them once they reach their mature size and color, but the longer you leave them to ripen, the hotter they will become.

Potatoes

You will need a large container that has good drainage for potatoes. It should be at least 16 inches (40 cm) deep and 16 inches (40 cm) wide, and you can plant 4–6 seed potatoes in a container this size.

Potatoes are grown from seed potatoes. A seed potato is a potato that is replanted and used to grow more potatoes. You can get them at a garden center. Make sure to get ones that are certified and disease-free. You can cut larger seed potatoes (larger than a chicken egg) that have multiple eye buds in half to grow more potatoes. When you're cutting, make sure that each side has at least 2 sprouts. Leave them for a few days after cutting so that the wound can heal, or they will rot otherwise. You can pre-sprout seed potatoes. This helps them develop sprouts, but it's not necessary. It's only required if you live in a climate that has short summers. To pre-sprout your seed potatoes, leave them in a cool and dark place for 2–3 weeks prior to planting.

Plant your seed potatoes after the last frost. To plant, fill the container with 6–8 inches (15–20 cm) of potting soil and place the seed potatoes in the container with the majority of the eyes facing upwards, spacing them a foot (30 cm) apart. After placing the seed potatoes, cover them with 6 inches (15 cm) of potting soil.

Potatoes grow best in full sun. They ideally need 8 hours of sunlight per day, but they can grow in partial sun too. Potatoes are a cool-season crop that grows best in temperatures between 60 and 70°F (15–21°C). Potatoes are perennial plants grown as annuals. Potato plants can grow up to 40 inches (1 m) tall, but most varieties usually grow up to 20 inches (50 cm) tall. Water potatoes regularly, and keep the soil evenly moist but not wet. You can add compost or well-rotted manure at the time of planting, and it should be enough for potatoes in terms of fertilizing. You can also fertilize them with a balanced liquid fertilizer once a month.

Potatoes usually take about 3 months to grow from planting to harvest. Wait until the tops of the vines have yellowed and started to die back before harvesting potatoes.

Pumpkins

Did you know that you can grow large pumpkins in containers? You will need a very larger container that can hold 20–25 gallons (76–95L) of soil, though. You can grow smaller varieties in a 10-gallon (38L) container.

You can start pumpkins indoors. Pumpkins don't transplant well, so I'd recommend sowing the seeds directly in the desired containers, but you can start them in a seed starting tray and transplant the seedlings into the desired containers after 3 weeks. Sow the seeds 3–4 weeks before the last frost. Plant them 1 inch (2.5 cm) deep, and water them so that the soil is moist but not soggy. You can move them outside 2–3 weeks after the last frost.

Pumpkins need full sun, ideally 8 hours of sunlight per day. Pumpkins are a warm-season crop that grows best in temperatures between 65 and 95°F (18–35°C). Pumpkins are annual plants. They can grow 10–30 inches (25–75 cm) tall and 4–16 feet (1.2–4.8 m) wide, so they will take a lot of space. Pumpkins need lots of water, so you'll have to water them frequently. You can mulch the container once the plants have grown a few inches tall. Pumpkins need to be fertilized every 2–3 weeks with a balanced or a low-nitrogen liquid fertilizer. Smaller pumpkin varieties will need a strong support, such as an A-shaped trellis.

Pumpkins usually take 3–4 months to grow from planting to harvesting. You can harvest them when they harden and take a uniform and intense color. You can press a pumpkin with your thumb to see if it's ready to be harvested. If the bark is hard and it sounds hollow—it's ready.

Radishes

Radishes need a container that is at least 6 inches (15 cm) deep, but if you have bought larger radishes, they may need an 8–10-inch (20–25 cm) deep container. Most radishes need 2 inches (5 cm) of spacing, so you'll need a wide container if you want to grow lots of radishes in one pot.

You can grow radishes from seed indoors. Sow the seeds 4–6 weeks before the last frost directly in the desired containers. Plant seeds ¼ to ½ an inch (0.6–1.2 cm) deep and 1 inch (2.5 cm) apart. They will germinate in 3–10 days, and you can move them outside when they have at least 2 sets of true leaves.

Radishes can grow in full or partial sun. They need at least 6 hours of sunlight per day. Radishes are a cool-season crop that grows best in temperatures between 55 and 65°F (13–18°C). Radishes can be either annual or biennial plants depending on the variety, but they are grown as annuals. Radish plants grow 6–18 inches (15–45 cm) tall and 6–9 inches (15–23 cm) wide. Radishes love moist soil, but don't overwater it so that it becomes soggy, and don't let it dry out completely.

Radishes don't need a lot of fertilizing. You can add compost or slow-release fertilizer at the time of planting and use a phosphorus-rich fertilizer, such as bone meal, a couple times during the growing season.

Radishes take 20–70 days to grow from planting to harvesting depending on the variety. Early maturing varieties can be harvested in 20–40 days, while Asian radish varieties take 40–70 days to grow until harvest. A good way to tell if your radishes are ready to be harvested is to simply pull one from the soil. You can harvest them when they're about 1 inch (2.5 cm) in diameter. You can also harvest radish tops. Harvest young and green leaves and use them in salads and soups.

Spinach

Spinach has a deep taproot, so if you want to grow it in containers, you'll need one that is at least 10 inches (25 cm) wide and deep.

You can start spinach indoors 6 weeks before the last frost and transplant it into containers outside right after the last frost. You can also direct sow spinach 4 weeks before the last frost. Plant the seeds ½ inch (1.2 cm) deep.

Spinach prefers full sun but can tolerate some shade. It needs at least 4 hours of sunlight per day; however, 4–6 hours is ideal. It's a cool-season crop, and it grows best in temperatures between 50 and 60°F (10–15°C). Spinach is an annual crop. Spinach needs to be watered regularly. You should fertilize spinach every 2–3 weeks during the growing season with a balanced liquid fertilizer.

Spinach is usually ready for harvest in 6–10 weeks. You can harvest leaves as needed or harvest an entire plant. When the outer leaves are about 6 inches (15 cm) long, they're ready to be harvested. Simply hold each leaf with one hand, and cut the stem with the other one. Harvest no more than 1/3 of a plant at once. If plants are near the end of the season, you can pull up or cut the entire plant.

Tomatoes

You will need a large container that is 24 inches (60 cm) deep and 20 inches (50 cm) in diameter to grow tomatoes. Some tomatoes will grow up to 6 feet (1.8 m) tall, so you will need stakes and maybe a trellis to help grow these up. Another thing to be aware of is how many tomatoes you actually want because all the tomatoes will need to be harvested at the same time, and you'll need to be ready to use them and preserve what you don't want to use immediately. So, it's worth having plenty of mason jars if you plan to grow lots of tomatoes.

Many people start with seedlings rather than seeds because they take a while to grow. If you decide to purchase seedlings, always get them from a reputable nursery. The plants should be dark green, short, and stocky with stems the size of a pencil or thicker. They should not have yellow leaves or spots.

If you decide to grow tomatoes from seed, then you need to sow these indoors 6 weeks before the last frost and put the seeds ½ inch (1.2 cm) deep in trays. Tomatoes can be placed in containers outdoors 2 weeks after the last frost. If you've grown them to seedlings, then do ensure you give the seedlings a week to get used to being outdoors, gradually increasing how long they remain outdoors each day before transplanting them into containers outside. The key warning, though, is not to put them outside too soon because tomatoes love warmth and will not withstand cold weather. You can either pinch off the bottom leaves when putting seedlings into containers or bury the stems up to the first good leaves if they're leggy.

Tomatoes need full sun, ideally at least 8 hours of sunlight per day. Tomatoes are a warm-season crop and they love warmth. They grow best in temperatures between 70 and 85°F (21–30°C). Tomatoes can be grown as perennials in their native tropical climate of South and Central America, but they are grown as annuals in other climates. Before tomatoes start to grow, you will see little yellow flowers. Tomatoes do need frequent watering—they typically need to be watered daily. It's best to water them first thing in the morning. Try to water them at the soil level and try not to splash the leaves. After 5 weeks, you could mulch the top of the soil to keep the soil cool and keep the moisture in. You will need to fertilize tomatoes every 2 weeks. You can get a fertilizer especially formulated for tomatoes, usually with a ratio like 3-4-6 or 4-7-10. You can pinch off small stems and leaves between branches and the main stem. You can stake tomato plants, and

I'd recommend doing that, as tomato plants can grow 3–10 ft (0.9–3 m) tall. You can also remove leaves from the bottom 12 inches (30 cm) of the stem.

Tomatoes can be harvested 60–100 days after planting. You can harvest them anytime they've begun to show a bit of color. Bring them indoors, and they'll ripen within a few days.

Zucchini

The perfect pot to grow zucchini in needs to be 14–18 inches (35–45 cm) wide and deep.

It is advised to sow zucchini seeds on their sides to reduce the chance of them rotting.

Zucchini plants have delicate roots and can be difficult to transplant, so I would suggest sowing the seeds directly in the desired containers. You can start zucchini indoors 4–6 weeks before the last frost and move the containers outside 1–2 weeks after the last frost. Make a 3/8-inch (1 cm) hole, then put 2 seeds in it, cover it, and then place the bottom half of a plastic bottle or a clear jar over the top to encourage the seed to grow.

Zucchini grow best in full sun. They need 6–8 hours of sunlight per day. It's a warm-season crop that grows best in temperatures above 70°F (21°C). Zucchini are annual plants. Zucchini plants can grow up to 2 feet (60 cm) in height and 2–3 feet (60–90 cm) wide. Zucchini do need plenty of space, and they enjoy sunshine. You want to protect them from strong winds. Zucchini don't need a lot of fertilizing. You should fertilize them with a balanced liquid fertilizer every 3–4 weeks during the growing season. If you added an A-shaped trellis, this would support the vines well and you could attach the vines to the trellis with ties.

Zucchini usually take 45–55 days to grow from seed to harvest. When you come to harvest them, remember that you can eat male zucchini flowers. You can fill and lightly batter them, but remember to leave some of these in order to pollinate the female flowers. Male flowers have a long, thin stem. Female flowers have a swollen base behind the flower—this is the ovary that later develops into a zucchini after germination. When you harvest zucchini, you can cut or twist them off. Smaller zucchini are denser and have a nutty taste. Bigger zucchini are waterier, so don't be tempted to grow your zucchini to a massive size before harvesting them. They taste better when they're smaller.

Fruits

Apples

You can grow dwarf varieties of apple trees in containers, and you'll need a container that is 18–22 inches (45–55 cm) in diameter and 10–15 gallons (38–57L) in volume.

Standard apple trees can grow 25–35 feet (7.5–10 m) tall, so they are too large for containers in most cases. You can get semi-dwarf and dwarf trees—they grow 6–20 feet (1.8–6 m tall). They will bloom and produce apples in the summer or fall. Apple trees need good air circulation so that leaves can dry and not attract fungus after it has rained. Dwarf varieties of apple trees need to be spaced 8 feet (2.4 m) apart, while full-sized trees need to be spaced 15 feet (4.5 m) apart.

If you want to grow apple trees from seed, you will have a really long wait, like 8–10 years before the trees would grow big enough to grow apples. You can buy apple trees from a nursery. If you do so, then it's best to buy more than one because most apple trees require another apple tree of a different variety nearby for cross-pollination to produce fruit. You can get self-pollinating apple trees, including self-pollinating dwarf apple trees, but they will produce more fruit if another tree is nearby for cross-pollination. It's also important to attract bees to your garden to help with pollination.

Apple trees like to be grown in full sun. They need to be watered 2–3 times a week during the growing season. They also need fertilizing every 2–3 weeks during the growing season with a balanced fertilizer.

Blueberries

You'll need a container that is at least 12 inches (30 cm) in diameter for blueberry bushes. Blueberries like acidic soil with a pH level between 4 and 5.5 pH, and it's best to water them with rainwater rather than tap water (which contains lime and can make soil more alkaline). You can buy potting mixes with this pH level, but they can be a bit more difficult to find. You can use potting mix for azaleas and rhododendrons to grow blueberry bushes in. As the plants grow, you may need to repot them into 20-inch (50 cm) containers. Blueberry bushes grow up to 4 feet (1.2

m) tall, and they spread to around 3 feet (90 cm). When you plant them, you should ensure they are spaced 5 feet (1.5 m) apart.

They prefer full sun, but they can grow in partial sun too. They need 6–8 hours of sunlight per day. Blueberries need to be watered regularly. If you plant two or more of these, they will do better than just a single plant. While they're growing, give them a liquid feed for acid-loving plants weekly. Blueberries respond well to any nitrogen-rich fertilizer, but they require fertilizers with an ammonium form of nitrogen, such as cottonseed meal. Any fertilizer sold for azaleas or rhododendrons also works well for blueberries.

For the first couple of years, you shouldn't need to prune blueberries. After this time, you can prune in February or March and get rid of one quarter of the older branches, keeping the newer ones. When you harvest blueberries, gently pick off the deepest blueberries. If any are green, allow them to fully ripen before picking them off. The more years go by, the greater the harvest you will get from them.

Cherries

Like with other fruit trees, you will need a large container. A 15-gallon (57L) container is enough for a tree that is 5 feet (1.5 m) tall. Standard cherry trees can grow up to 35 feet (10 m) tall, so naturally they'll be too large for containers, but you can get dwarf varieties that grow 6.5– 8 feet (2–2.5 m) tall but still produce full-sized fruit.

You can grow a cherry tree from cuttings, seeds, or pits, but it will take years until it matures. They can start producing fruit after 2 years, but will reach full cropping between 4 and 5 years, so I would suggest buying a tree from a nursery. There are two main varieties of cherry trees—sweet and sour. Sweet cherries are usually eaten, and sour cherries are typically used for cooking or baking. Sweet cherry trees need to be spaced 35–40 (10.7–12.2 m) feet apart, and their dwarf varieties need 5–10 feet (1.5–3 m) of space. Sour cherry trees need to be spaced 20–25 feet (6–7.6 m) apart, and their dwarf varieties need 8–10 feet (2.4–3 m) of space.

Cherry trees need full sun, ideally 6–8 hours of sunlight per day. Young cherry trees need to be watered 3–5 times per week, while mature trees need to be watered only 2–3 times per week.

Cherry trees don't need a lot of fertilizing—you can use a low-nitrogen fertilizer in the spring 2–3 weeks before the tree blossoms, and then fertilize them every 4–6 weeks during the growing season. You should prune cherry trees once a year, but try to do it in the warmer months because pruning in the winter makes the tree more vulnerable to diseases.

Figs

Fig trees require a 15–20-gallon (57–76L) container. They take 3–5 years to mature, so like with other fruit trees, I'd suggest buying a tree from a nursery. They grow 10–30 feet (3–10 m), but you can get dwarf trees that grow 4–6 feet (1.2–1.8 m) tall. Full-size trees need to be spaced 12–25 feet (3.6–7.6 m) apart, and dwarf trees need to be spaced 8 feet (2.4 m) apart.

Fig trees need full sun, ideally 7–8 hours of sunlight per day. They need to be watered 2–3 times a week. Fig trees are more tolerant of dry soil than wet soil. Yellow foliage and dropping leaves are signs of underwatering. You can fertilize them with a balanced fertilizer once a month, beginning when the tree starts to put on new leaves and stopping before the end of July.

If you're growing fig trees in containers, I would suggest moving your fig trees indoors for the winter. You can place them in an unheated garage or a basement. Once they're indoors, reduce watering significantly. Only water them when the top 2 inches (5 cm) of the container are dry. You can move them back outside in the spring after the last frost, gradually introducing them to outdoor conditions over the course of a few weeks.

Gooseberries

You can grow gooseberry bushes in containers. You will need a 10-gallon (38L) container to grow a gooseberry bush. Gooseberry bushes tend to grow to a height of 5 feet (1.5 m) and are about 5 feet (1.5 m) wide. They need to be spaced 4–5 feet (1.2–1.5 m) apart with 6–8 feet (1.8 m–2.4 m) between rows. They will give you berries for 15 years, and you can expect a yield of 7–8 lb (3–3.6 kg) from each bush.

You can grow gooseberry bushes from seed; however, they are commonly sold as dormant bare-root or live potted plants, and I'd suggest going that route. It's best to plant gooseberry bushes in the spring. You can grow gooseberry bushes up trellises, walls, or fences. It's worth thinning out the bush in June and getting rid of some gooseberries the size of a pea at this point. If you need to prune the bush, do this once a year to give it a goblet shape. You may decide to put nets over the bushes when the berries are starting to ripen to prevent birds from eating them.

Gooseberries prefer full sun but can grow in partial sun too. Ideally, they need 8 hours of sunlight per day. They need to be watered regularly. Gooseberries typically need to be fertilized twice a year with a balanced fertilizer—once in early spring, just as the buds begin to swell, and again in midsummer, after the fruit has set. You can prune them once a year, and it's best to do it in the winter or early spring before new growth starts to sprout. Gooseberry bushes tolerate temperatures below freezing well, so you can leave them outside over the winter if you're growing them in containers.

Lemons

You can grow smaller lemon trees in a 5-gallon (19L) container, but for larger trees you'll need at least a 10-gallon (38L) container. Lemon trees grow 10–20 feet (3–6 m) tall, but you can get dwarf varieties that stay under 10 feet (3 m) tall, usually 3–5 feet (0.9–1.5 m) tall.

I'd suggest buying lemon trees from a nursery, as it takes 3–6 years to grow a lemon tree from seed to maturity, but you can grow them from cuttings or from seed. If you decide to grow from seed, you could let the seed dry out for a couple of weeks. Then when it's dry, put it into the soil an inch (2.5 cm) deep and cover with plastic wrap. Let the seedling get to 10 inches (25 cm) before you transplant it outside. Lemon trees should be spaced 12–25 feet (3.6–7.6 m) apart, while dwarf varieties need to be spaced 6–10 feet (1.8–3 m) apart.

Lemon trees need full sun. They need 8 hours of sunlight to grow. They need to be watered 2–3 times per week in the summer. Lemon trees should be fertilized with a balanced fertilizer only when there is active growth, so you can fertilize them from spring right before flowering and until the start of fall every 2–3 weeks. Lemon trees are quite sensitive to the cold, and freezing temperatures can damage or even kill them. If you're growing them in containers, you could bring them indoors over the winter.

Melons

You can grow full-sized melons in containers, although they will often outgrow the containers they are in. You'll get the best results with dwarf cultivars that produce smaller fruit and shorter vines. You'll need a container that is at least 16 inches (40 cm) deep and 14 inches (35 cm) wide or 5 gallons (19 L) in volume.

Melons are best started indoors 4 weeks before the last frost date. You can transplant them to containers outside a week after the last frost. In warmer climates, you can direct sow melons 1–2 weeks after the last frost. Plant the seeds ½ to 1 inch (1.2–2.5 cm) deep.

Melons need full sun—at least 8 hours of sunlight per day. They are a warm-season crop, and they grow best in temperatures between 65 and 95°F (18–35°C). Melons are annual plants. You'll need to water melon plants daily. Melons need to be fertilized every 2–3 weeks during the growing season. Phosphorus- and potassium-rich fertilizers are best, but a balanced fertilizer will work fine too.

Melons usually take 80–90 days to grow to maturity after transplanting. Harvest when fruits produce their characteristic melon fragrance and start to crack near the stem. A fully ripe melon will separate from the vine with light pressure. You can also cut melons from the vine with a sharp knife. Leave an inch (2.5 cm) of stem attached to the fruit to keep it from rotting if you don't plan to use the harvested melon immediately.

Peaches and Nectarines

You can grow smaller trees in a 5-gallon (19L) container, but you'll need a 10–15-gallon (38–57L) container for larger trees. Unlike apple trees, peach trees have no dwarf rootstock to keep the trees small. Instead, some varieties naturally grow smaller. They are called natural dwarfs, and they produce full-sized fruit. They grow 6–10 feet (1.8–3 m) tall. There are also small nectarine trees. Dwarf trees should be spaced 10–12 feet (3–3.6 m) apart.

Like with other fruit trees, I'd suggest getting a tree from a nursery because peach trees can take 3–4 years to mature. They need full sun, ideally 8 hours of sunlight per day. You need to water them deeply every few days when the soil dries out. You only need to start fertilizing them when they begin bearing fruit, which usually takes 3–4 years. Mature trees should be fertilized every 2–3 weeks with a balanced fertilizer only during the growing season. Most peach trees grow compact and don't require pruning. You can prune them if they start getting a bit too large.

Raspberries

You'll need a container that's 16–20 inches (40–50 cm) wide and deep for a raspberry bush.

You can purchase one-year-old raspberry canes from a nursery to plant them. One bush alone can provide you with hundreds of berries in a season. Ideally, plant them in the spring, and they will bloom in the summer or fall. It's best to soak the roots of the plant for a couple of hours before planting. Raspberry canes should be spaced 18 inches (45 cm) apart. Generally, raspberries will produce fruit a year after you have planted the bush. You will need to prune the bush every year.

Raspberries like to grow in full sun. They need 6–8 hours of sunlight per day. The more sun the bush gets, the more raspberries it will produce. They need to be watered 2–3 times per week. You should fertilize them a few times during the growing season with a balanced fertilizer. You can also give your raspberry bushes some compost or aged manure every year. They grow 4–8 feet (1.2–2.4 m) tall and 3–5 feet (0.9–1.5 m) wide. You can cut the canes down to 9 inches (23 cm) tall after planting, which will encourage new growth. You may need supports to keep the canes in place. You could use a trellis or a fence.

After you have harvested your berries, cut the canes that produced them back to the ground. Prune only the old canes (the brown stems that produced berries), and leave the younger green canes. You can tie canes to supports with strings. When it comes to harvesting berries, you'll need to pick them every few days. Try to collect them when it's dry, and you shouldn't need to pull too hard. When they're ripe, it shouldn't be difficult to remove them from the vine.

Strawberries

You can grow individual strawberry plants in containers that are 6–8 inches (15–20 cm) deep and wide. You can grow multiple plants in one container if you space them 10–12 inches (25–30 cm) apart.

Strawberries are best started from seed indoors. You can start them indoors 8 weeks before the last frost. Sow the seeds thinly and press them into the growing medium. They can take anywhere between 1 and 6 weeks to germinate. You can transplant the seedlings to containers outside after the last frost when they have 3 sets of true leaves. Don't bury the crown of the plant when you plant it. The crown should be at the surface of the soil so that it doesn't rot.

Strawberries like to be grown in full sun. They need 6–8 hours of sunlight per day. Strawberries are short-term perennials that continuously replicate and renew themselves, and they can be productive for 4–5 years, but they can also be grown as annuals that you replant each year. They grow 6–8 inches (15–20 cm) tall and 12 inches (30 cm) wide. You can mulch the soil to help retain moisture and keep the soil cool. Strawberries need to be watered when the top 1 inch (2.5 cm) of soil feels dry. You can fertilize them with a balanced fertilizer every 3 weeks during the growing season. After the flowers have appeared, you can fertilize them, and you should get ripe berries approximately 30 days after that.

When your strawberries bloom depends on what type of strawberry plants you've purchased. If you have got June-bearing strawberries, then you will need to harvest all the fruit in one go over 3 weeks. Everbearing strawberries will produce most of the crop in the spring and some throughout the summer and then another crop in late summer or early fall. Day-neutral varieties will produce fruit all throughout the season until the first frost. I personally like June-bearing strawberries, and while you'll need to wait a year until your first harvest, they taste incredibly delicious, and it's worth the wait.

It is advisable that in the first year you pick off the flowers—this will discourage the plant from fruiting and will help focus its energy on building strong roots instead. This will help you have a bigger yield of berries the following year. If you live in a very cold area, once the strawberries have finished, you can cut the plants down to one inch (2.5 cm), and place 4 inches (10 cm) of mulch on them. You can remove the mulch in early spring after the last frost.

Herbs

Basil

You'll need a container that's 10–12 inches (20–25 cm) deep to grow basil.

Basil is my favorite herb, and I absolutely adore it. I love the smell, and it's so versatile—it can add such a boost of flavor to many dishes. You can get a variety of flavors of basil: sweet, purple, lemon, and Thai. You can start growing basil indoors 6 weeks before the last frost. The plant does like warmth, and it won't grow well without it. When you sow basil seeds, put them ¼ inch (6 mm) deep. You can transplant the seedlings to containers outside 1–2 weeks after the last frost when they've grown 3 pairs of true leaves.

Basil prefers to grow in full sun with 6–8 hours of sunlight per day, but it can grow in partial shade too. Basil in an annual herb. It grows to about 12–24 inches (30–60 cm) in height. You can put mulch on the soil to keep the moisture in and keep the soil cool. Basil needs to be watered every 2–3 days. If the weather is hot, the plants will want a lot of water. You can fertilize basil every 2–3 weeks with a balanced liquid fertilizer. If you know there will be a bad frost, harvest the basil before this because the cold will destroy basil plants.

Basil usually takes 3–4 weeks to grow from planting to harvest. When the plants are 8 inches (20 cm) tall, they are ready to harvest. It's best to harvest basil in the morning. Picking the leaves will encourage more growth. If you don't need them immediately, you can store them to use when required by freezing or drying the leaves.

Chives

You'll need a container that is 6–8 inches (15–20 cm) deep for chives, and you can grow multiple plants in one container if you space them 6 inches (15 cm) apart.

Chives look very pretty when they're growing because of their lovely purple flowers. They also smell and taste fantastic and can really enhance the taste of many dishes, giving them that wonderful onion taste but without the need to cut up an onion. The plant will grow up to 12 inches (30 cm) tall, and they will spread to around 10 inches (25 cm). Chives are a perennial herb, and I've always found them incredibly resilient—they spring back up year after year.

They're a perfect herb for containers. Growing chives from seed is quite easy. Sow the seeds a month before the last frost and plant them ¼ inch (0.6 cm) deep. They germinate best on a heat pad or a warm windowsill. The seedlings should grow within three weeks, and there's no need to thin these out, unless the pot is really crowded. When they reach 2 inches (5 cm) in height, you can put them into 8-inch (20 cm) pots and continue growing these. You can transplant the seedlings to containers outside 1–2 weeks after the last frost.

Chives grow best in full sun with 6–8 hours of sunlight per day, but they can grow in partial shade too. Keep them watered regularly and make sure the soil is moist but not soggy. You can fertilize them every 4–6 weeks with a balanced liquid fertilizer.

Chives take 60 days to grow from seed to harvest. When you harvest chives, it's best to cut leaves from the base of the plant with a pair of scissors. Don't eat the stems of flowering shoots.

Dill

Dill has a long tap root, so you'll need a container that is at least 12 inches (30 cm) deep and wide.

You can grow dill from seed but not from cuttings. Sow the seeds directly into the desired pots a month before the last frost. They will germinate in 7–10 days. You can move them outdoors once the plants are 4–6 inches (10–15 cm) tall and the danger of frost has passed.

Dill grows best in full sun with 6–8 hours of sunlight per day. Dill is an annual herb. It can grow 2–4 feet (0.6–1.2 m) tall. Keep the soil evenly moist, but don't let it get soggy. Dill doesn't need lots of fertilizing. A light feeding of a phosphorus-rich or a balanced liquid fertilizer applied once in late spring should be enough.

Dill is usually ready for harvest 90 days after planting. To harvest, snip the stems of the leaves right where they meet the growth point on the main stem with a pair of scissors.

Lemon Verbena

You'll need a container that is at least 12 inches (30 cm) deep and wide for lemon verbena.

Lemon verbena has a lovely citrus aroma. It's great to give a lemony flavor to a wide variety of dishes. You can use it fresh or dry it. It's a fast-growing herb, and it will have the best taste if it grows in full sun.

Lemon verbena is quite difficult to grow from seed, so I would suggest getting a plant from a nursery and then propagating new plants from it via cuttings. You can plant lemon verbena in the spring right after the last frost. The plants should be planted 12–16 inches (30–40 cm) apart.

Lemon verbena grows best in full sun with 6–8 hours of sunlight per day. Lemon verbena can be grown as a perennial in frost-free climates, but it's grown as an annual in colder climates. Try to ensure that no other plants or trees are casting shade onto it. Lemon verbena needs to be watered regularly. If you don't water it regularly, the plant becomes stressed and will drop its leaves. The soil should be moist but not soggy. This is an herb that enjoys regular fertilizing. You can fertilize it every 2–4 weeks with a balanced liquid fertilizer during the growing season. Compost or manure tea also works well. It will bloom in late summer. It is worth noting that this is an herb that can be toxic to cats, dogs, and horses, so it's probably best not to grow it if you have any of these animals. It can grow up to 6 feet (1.8 m) tall. You could grow this up a wall, a fence, or a trellis.

Lemon verbena can be harvested as needed or as a whole plant. You can start harvesting once the plant has several leaves and has reached a height of about 10 inches (25 cm). When it comes to harvesting this herb, don't just pluck leaves off a stem. Cut back a stem to a quarter of an inch (6 mm) near a leaf or a node. Don't take more than a quarter of the stem so that the plant can keep on growing. If the plant has become really tall, you can cut it back by a third in early spring to make it more compact. If you live somewhere cold, cut the plant back to a few inches above ground in the winter and then cover it with 5 inches (12.5 cm) of mulch.

Mint

For mint, you'll need a container that's 10–12 inches (25–30 cm) deep and wide.

You can grow mint from seed; however, germination is undependable. I'd suggest getting a mint plant from a nursery, and then you can propagate it via cuttings. If you decide to grow from seed, sow the seeds 8–10 weeks before the last frost directly in the desired containers and plant them ¼ inch (0.6 cm) deep. They will germinate in 7–14 days. You can move the seedlings outside after the last frost.

Mint can grow in either full or partial sun, but it grows best in full sun with 6–8 hours of sunlight per day. Mint is a perennial herb. It can grow 12–18 inches (30–45 cm) tall. You can add slow-release fertilizer during planting. Keep the soil evenly moist and don't let it dry out. Mint doesn't need a lot of fertilizing. You can use a balanced fertilizer in the spring when new growth emerges and then fertilize it every 4–6 weeks after that.

Mint takes 90 days to grow from planting to harvest. It's best to harvest mint leaves right before flowers appear. You can start harvesting individual leaves as needed when the plants reach at least 4 inches (10 cm) in height.

Oregano

You'll need a container that's 10–12 inches (25–30 cm) deep and wide for oregano.

You can start oregano from seed indoors. Sow the seeds directly in the desired containers 4 weeks before the last frost. For some varieties, you don't need to cover the seeds with soil— you can simply sprinkle them on the surface of the soil. Your seed packet should have information on how deep to plant the seeds. Seeds usually take 10–15 days to germinate. You can move the seedlings outdoors 1–2 weeks after the last frost.

Oregano prefers to grow in full sun with 6–8 hours of sunlight per day. Oregano is a perennial herb. It can grow up to 2 feet (60 cm) tall and 18 inches (45 cm) wide. The more sun it gets, the stronger the flavor will be. Water oregano moderately—only water it when the surface of the soil is dry. Oregano typically doesn't need a lot of fertilizing. You can add some compost during planting. Other than that, you won't need to do much else in terms of fertilizing. If you have a bushier plant, you can prune it once it's at least 4 inches (10 cm) tall. Pinch the top part along with the first set of leaves and just above the leaf node. This will make your plant grow thick and lush.

Oregano usually takes 45 days to grow from planting to harvesting. You can start harvesting leaves as needed once the plant is at least 6 inches (15 cm) tall. Never harvest more than 2/3 of all leaves. Oregano loses flavor after flowering, so it's best to harvest it before it starts flowering.

Parsley

For parsley, you'll need a container that is 10 inches (25 cm) wide and deep.

You can start parsley indoors 6–10 weeks before the last frost. Soaking the seeds in water for 12–24 hours before planting can help with germination. Plant the seeds ¼ inch (0.6 cm) deep. They can be a bit finicky, so you can plant 2–3 seeds in each container. They will germinate in 14–28 days. Parsley is frost hardy, so you can move it outside 2–4 weeks before the last frost, but I would suggest waiting until after the last frost, just in case.

Parsley grows well in full and partial sun. It needs at least 6 hours of sunlight per day. Parsley is a biennial herb grown as an annual. It can grow 9–12 inches (23–30 cm) tall and wide. It needs regular watering—keep the soil slightly moist but not wet. Parsley doesn't need a lot of fertilizing. You can add compost or aged manure at the time of planting or use a phosphorus-rich or a balanced liquid fertilizer once or twice during the growing season. You can remove the flower stalks, and this should help the plant focus on foliage growth instead. You can also pick dead, faded, and yellowed leaves from time to time.

Parsley typically takes 70–90 days to grow from planting to harvest. You can start harvesting parsley leaves as needed 2–3 months after planting. Wait until the stems are divided into three sections before harvesting. Instead of only picking the leaves from the top, cut the entire stem carefully from the base—parsley stems are also edible and tasty.

Rosemary

Rosemary needs some space for its roots to expand, so you'll need a container that is at least 12 inches (30 cm) wide and deep.

Rosemary is rather difficult to grow from seed. The germination rate is quite low, and it will take months until the plant can produce usable leaves. It's much easier to grow rosemary from cuttings, so I'd suggest getting a plant from a nursery and then propagating it via cuttings.

Rosemary likes to grow in full sun with 6–8 hours of sunlight per day. Rosemary is a perennial shrub. Rosemary can grow quite big, so if you put it in a container, it could be that in a few years it will need to be transplanted into a bigger container. It can grow up to 4 feet (1.2 m) tall. Rosemary doesn't like sitting in moist or wet soil, so water it only when the top 2 inches (5 cm) of the soil are dry or about once a week. Rosemary doesn't need a lot of fertilizing. You can add compost or a balanced slow-release fertilizer at the time of planting and then fertilize it with a balanced liquid fertilizer once a month during the growing season. You can cut back the plant if it's starting to become woody. In the fall, you can mulch the top of the soil.

Rosemary takes 80–100 days to grow from planting to harvest if you grow it from cuttings. If you grow it from seed, it can take a year to grow to maturity. You can harvest rosemary by pulling sprigs off the main stem. If you need large branches to roast, then you could use secateurs to remove these. You can dry rosemary, but you can't freeze it.

Sage

For sage, you'll need a container that's 10 inches (25 cm) wide and deep.

You can grow sage from seed, but just like rosemary, sage is rather difficult to grow from seed. I'd suggest getting a plant from a local nursery, and then you can propagate it via cuttings.

Sage is an herb that likes to be grown in full sun with 6–8 hours of sunlight per day. Sage can be an annual or a perennial herb depending on your climate. It can be grown as a perennial in colder to moderate climates and as an annual in hotter climates. Young plants need watering often so that they don't dry out. Once the plant develops, keep it on the drier side—only water when the soil is dry to the touch. Sage doesn't need a lot of fertilizing. In fact, overfertilizing it can result in weaker flavor. You can add compost at the time of planting or use a balanced liquid fertilizer once every 4–6 weeks during the growing season. Sage plants can grow 12–30 inches (30–75 cm) tall. If plants become woody, you can prune them. You need to give sage plants a good pruning every year. It's best to do it when new growth starts to appear, young leaves unfurl, and new buds form in the spring. Sage plants need replacing every couple of years to remain productive.

Sage typically takes 75 days to grow from cuttings to harvest. To harvest sage, you can pinch off some leaves or sprigs from it. Try not to harvest too much from the plants in the first year. When the plant is fully established, you can harvest it three times in a growing season. Don't harvest it in the fall so that the plant can prepare for winter. Fresh sage tastes best, but you can freeze or dry it. If you're drying it, hang sprigs in a warm area and allow to air dry.

Thyme

Thyme doesn't need a large container—a container that's 6–8 inches (15–20 cm) deep and wide is more than enough.

You can grow thyme from seed or cuttings. You can start seeds 6–10 weeks before the last frost. You can plant them directly in the desired containers ¼ inch (0.6 cm) deep. They usually take around 28 days to germinate, and you can move the seedlings outside after the last frost. Or you can save yourself the hassle of growing from seed and get a plant from a nursery and then propagate it via cuttings.

Thyme prefers to grow in full sun with 6–8 hours of sunlight per day. Thyme is a perennial herb. It can grow up to 6–12 inches (15–30 cm) tall. It's an herb that doesn't need too much water. Water it deeply when the topsoil is dry. Thyme doesn't need a lot of fertilizing. You can add compost or a slow-release balanced fertilizer at the time of planting and then fertilize it with a balanced liquid fertilizer every 6–8 weeks during the growing season. Typically, the plants will grow 6–12 inches (15–30 cm) tall. If you want to plant something near it, you could plant rosemary which has similar water requirements. You can leave thyme outside over the winter, and new leaves will come up in spring. In early spring, you can fertilize it with compost. You can prune it back in the spring and summer. If you've had the plant for 3–4 years, you may want to replace it, as it may not taste as flavorful.

You can harvest thyme all year round, but to get the most flavor, harvest it just before it starts flowering. Cut only a few stems in the first year. Many gardeners don't harvest thyme in the first year at all. It's best to cut off the top 5–6 inches (12.5–15 cm) when you harvest this and do it in the morning. Don't wash it because doing so will remove the essential oils. You can freeze it or dry the leaves in the oven or by hanging them.

Flowers

Geraniums

You'll need a container that's 12 inches (30 cm) in diameter for geraniums. These flowers thrive in terracotta pots. You can grow geraniums in hanging baskets too.

You can get edible scented-leaf geraniums. Geraniums come in pink, red, purple, bronze, and white. You can start geraniums from seed. Geraniums take 12–16 weeks to grow from planting to blooming. You can sow the seeds 10 weeks before the last frost. Plant them ¼ inch (0.6 cm) deep. You can start taking them outside when the weather begins to warm after the last frost.

Geraniums need full or partial sun depending on the variety. Annual geraniums need the most sun. Geraniums are usually grown as annuals, but they can be grown as perennials in warmer climates. They can grow 4–48 inches (10–120 cm) tall and 6–36 inches (15–90 cm) wide. They need to be watered 2–3 times per week. You can fertilize them every 2–4 weeks with a balanced liquid fertilizer during active growth in the spring and summer. Cut the plants back late summer, and it's worth taking cuttings in case you have

any losses. It's best to move containers with geraniums indoors over the winter and bring them out again in May. When planting geraniums, they like peat-free all-purpose potting mix with a slow-release fertilizer. Throughout the summer, they will need watering well, and if you deadhead flowers, then more will grow.

Marigolds

Container size will depend on the variety you're growing. Smaller varieties, such as French or Signet, need a 6–8-inch (15–20 cm) container, while larger one, like African or Mexican, need a 12-inch (30 cm) container.

Marigold seeds are easy to germinate, and they will bloom in 8 weeks. If growing from seed, sow them 1 inch (2.5 cm) apart 4–6 weeks before the last frost and water them thoroughly. Thin them and plant them out 10 inches (25 cm) apart. You can start seeds in trays or directly in the growing containers because they germinate fast. You can move them outdoors after the last frost.

Marigolds are a beautiful, vibrant orange color, and they are an asset to any garden. They also attract pollinators and beneficial insects, such as butterflies, bees, and ladybugs.

Marigolds can grow in full or partial sun. They need 5–6 hours of sunlight per day. Most marigolds are annuals, but some varieties are perennials. Most varieties of marigolds are self-seeding, so they may appear to be perennials, but in reality, they are just coming back from seed. They can grow 6–18 inches (15–45 cm) tall.

Marigolds need to be watered when the top 1–2 inches (2.5–5cm) of the soil are dry. They typically don't need fertilizing, especially if your soil has been enriched with compost, but you can fertilize them occasionally with a balanced liquid fertilizer. They will bloom from late spring and until fall. They are great flowers for beginners to grow. They can be planted near vegetables, and it will help deter pests and attract pollinators and beneficial insects. You can deadhead marigolds flowers, which will make the plant look better and encourage further growth. It's best to water marigolds from the base rather than overhead because flower heads can rot.

There is a wide variety of marigolds available all in warm, sunny colors. They can be from 6 inches (15 cm) to 4 feet (15 cm–1.2 m) tall and from 6 inches (15 cm) to 2 feet (15–60 cm) wide. French marigolds are the most common type. There are also tall African marigolds and Signet marigolds, which are edible and can be used in salads and pastas. If you're growing the taller African marigolds, you should plant them in early spring after the last frost because they take

longer to grow and mature. But other types can be planted any time in the spring or summer. The taller varieties need to be protected from strong winds and may need a support stake.

Nasturtiums

You'll need a 10–12-inch (25–30 cm) container for nasturtiums.

You can start nasturtiums from seed. They don't transplant well because they have delicate roots, so it's best to start them directly in the desired containers. Sow the seeds indoors 2–4 weeks before the last frost. Plant the seeds ¼ to ½ inch (0.6–1.2 cm) deep. The seeds will take 10–12 days to germinate. You can move the containers outside after the last frost.

Nasturtiums do best in full sun. They need 6–8 hours of sunlight per day. They are an annual plant. Nasturtiums are fast growing and easy to look after. They need to be watered when the top 2 inches (5 cm) of soil are dry or about once a week. They don't tend to need fertilizing. If you fertilize them, it will increase foliage growth but won't help increase flower growth. There are many different types of nasturtiums, including bushy plants, trailing plants, and climbers, so if you like these, you can add a variety of different types to your container garden. The leaves and flowers are edible, and they have a peppery taste. Depending on the type you buy, they can be 1–10 feet (30 cm–3 m) tall, and 1–3 feet (30–90 cm) wide. They bloom from May to September.

Pansies

You'll need a container that is 12 inches (30 cm) for pansies.

They can be quite difficult to start from seed, so I would suggest getting a plant from a nursery. If you want to start them from seed, surface sow the seeds in a seed starting tray 8–10 weeks before the last frost and cover them with a clear plastic cover or food wrap. Remove it once the seeds have germinated. Pansy seeds usually take 7–10 days to germinate. You can transplant them once they are a few inches tall, and you can move them outside after the last frost.

Pansies can grow in full or partial sun. They need 6 hours of sunlight per day. Pansies are short-season perennials, but they are usually grown as annuals. They can be grown as biennials in climates with mild winters. They can grow 6–9 inches (15–23 cm) tall and 9–12 inches (23–30 cm) wide. You need to water them when the top ½ inch (1.2 cm) of the soil is dry. You can fertilize them with a balanced liquid fertilizer every 2–3 weeks. You can leave them outside in the winter. Give your pansies a good watering before a hard freeze. You can cover them during extremely cold weather.

Petunias

You can grow 3 petunia plants in a 12-inch (30 cm) container, or you can grow individual plants in 6–8-inch (15–20 cm) containers.

If you wish to grow them from seed, start the seeds indoors 8–10 weeks before the last frost. Plant the seeds ¼ inch (0.6 cm) deep. Petunia seeds are tiny and will need lots of light to germinate. You can transplant the seedlings outside after the last frost, but they'll need to be protected from any frosts that may occur.

There are many different types of petunias that differ in size, multifloras being perhaps the most common. Grandifloras have large flowers. Floribundas have medium-sized flowers. Millifloras are very small, and you can get spreading or trailing petunias too. It is easy to buy young petunias from a nursery, but make sure the plants you buy are not too leggy.

Petunias prefer full sun. They need at least 6 hours of sunlight per day. Petunias can be grown as perennials in frost-free climates, but they are typically grown as annuals. They need frequent watering. You should water them when the top 1 inch (2.5 cm) of the soil feels dry or daily in most cases. Petunias should be fertilized once a month with a balanced liquid fertilizer to help encourage them to grow and bloom. If you prune them, it's advisable to fertilize them afterwards. If they look scruffy, they will soon grow more flowers and look better. You can deadhead old flowers, and this will make them look more attractive.

They will bloom in the spring, summer, and fall. Petunias come in a wide range of colors. They flower for a long time, which means they are plants that give you good value for money and make your garden look great. Midway through the summer they may get leggy, and you'll need to prune them back to half their height. They can grow 6–18 inches (15–45 cm) tall, and their spread can be between 18 inches and 4 feet (0.45–1.2 m).

My personal favorite plants to grow are tomatoes. I just think they're incredibly versatile. They're tangy, sweet, and have a rich taste. You can use them in salads, eat them as a snack, make soups out of them, and make delicious sauces for pizzas, pastas, and other dishes. But I also love the great variety of vegetables, fruits, herbs, and flowers that we grow. They all bring something to our table in terms of flavor, great nutrition, vitamins, and help us live a healthy, organic, and sustainable lifestyle.

Key takeaways from this chapter:

1. Whether buying seeds or seedlings, be certain to check all plant information thoroughly to see how big the plant will grow (and therefore you can judge what size container to put them in), whether they need full sun (which will help you to know where to place the container), the soil type they require, when to plant them, how deep to plant the seeds, how far apart you should space them, and when to prune them.

2. You may need to thin seeds out to give the strongest ones room to grow.

3. Some plants, such as carrots, don't like to be transplanted, so plant them directly in the containers you'll grow them in. Whereas other plants need to be grown indoors and then transplanted into containers when ready—check this before purchasing.

4. Mulch the top of the soil to retain moisture, reduce weeds, and to keep the soil and plants' roots cool.

5. Plants in containers need to be fertilizer with a liquid fertilizer during the growing season.

6. You may need to provide support for some plants that grow tall or climbing plants. You can use stakes, canes, fences, or trellises to provide support for plants that need it.

7. Many vegetables and fruits taste better when they're smaller, so there's no need to grow them to a huge size.

8. Try to avoid getting water on leaves because this can cause fungus, mold, and rot. Water your plants at the base instead.

9. Remember that dwarf varieties are a great option if you don't have a lot of space.

10. Some plants, like sage, will need to be replaced after a few years because they won't be as flavorful with time.

Conclusion

There are so many different types of vegetables, fruits, herbs, and flowers that you can choose to grow in containers. Container gardening really can transform your life. It can give you an amazing, relaxing, and enjoyable hobby that can provide you with having a lovely selection of freshly grown vegetables and fruits. Growing your own food can help you live a healthier and more sustainable lifestyle. You know that it is organic with no harmful pesticides because you've personally grown and nurtured it. And it tastes delicious! You can make incredible meals from the produce you've personally grown as well as baked goods, jams, chutneys, pickles, and much more.

So, this book is for beginners who are interested in container gardening. It is a complete guide on how to grow vegetables, fruits, herbs, and flowers in containers. This book has outlined the benefits and drawbacks of container gardening. I think the drawbacks are negligible, compared to the many benefits we get. I am addicted to container gardening, and all my friends and family know that they can buy me beautiful, glazed containers, or potting soil, or seeds for any gifts, and I'll be thrilled.

The chapters of the book have taken you through the different container types you have available and how to choose the right pot for the plants you want to grow. You'll know how to choose the perfect location for your container garden and how to consider the space. You'll need to consider what sunlight the area gets, whether it's sheltered or not, how easy it is to get water to the plants, and how accessible the space is for you. You'll have considered how to make your garden have a design that you love using different styles of containers and a variety of things like hanging baskets, planting at different heights, using trailing plants, vertical planters, climbers, and so on. You've also learned what makes a good potting soil, how to choose potting soil for your plants and how to mix your own potting soil.

As you've moved through the book, information has been given about the options of whether you grow plants from seed or purchase seedlings. There are pros and cons to both, and it's entirely your choice. A chapter of the book has covered garden maintenance to ensure that you know how to take care of your plants, how to water your garden properly, how you can make this easier, and what to do if you need to go on holiday. There is information about turning containers, deadheading and pruning plants, keeping the garden tidy, repotting plants, and looking after your container garden over the winter months.

There is a chapter of the book that looks at dealing with pests and diseases that could affect your container garden. This chapter includes tips on how to spot these pests and how to deal with them. The book covers information on when to harvest your vegetables, fruits, and herbs, and how to store them for later use. The final chapter covers plant profiles to provide you information about the plants you might want to grow so that you have a good indication as to how big the plants will grow, their sun requirements, whether they're grown from seeds or seedlings, how much water or fertilizer they require, and more.

Now that you've reached the end of the book, my advice would be to take a good look at what space you have available. Then make a list of the vegetables, fruits, and herbs that you enjoy eating, and see whether the space you have gives you optimum conditions for growing some of your favorite produce. Then buy your containers, potting mix, and either seeds or seedlings, and get started on what I think is one of the most rewarding hobbies in the world!

Resources

Choosing the Right Container for Your Plants

Deike, Chloe. 2020. Pros & Cons of Different Types of Garden Containers. *Garden Gate Magazine*. 17th July 2020. Online.

https://www.gardengatemagazine.com/articles/containers/all/different-types-of-garden-containers/

Iannotti, Marie. 2020. How to Choose the Right Garden Planter, Container, or Pot. *The Spruce*. Online. 26th Jan 2020. https://www.thespruce.com/before-you-buy-a-garden-planter-1402344

Melissa. 2022. Types of Containers for Container Gardening Vegetables. *Living a Frugal Life*. Online. https://www.livingafrugallife.com/types-of-containers-for-container-gardens/

Tilley, Nikki. 2021. Choosing Containers for Potted Environments. *Gardening Know How*. 26th July, 2021. Online. https://www.gardeningknowhow.com/special/containers/choosing-containers-for-potted-environments.htm

University of Illinois Extension. 2022. Making Herb and Vegetable Containers. *University of Illinois Extension*. Online.

https://web.extension.illinois.edu/containergardening/herbveggie_containers.cfm

Vinje, E. 2022. Selecting Pots for Plants. *Planet Natural Research Center*. Online. https://www.planetnatural.com/selecting-a-container/

Choosing the Perfect Location for Your Container Garden

Bouffard, Marie. 2017. How to Start a Container Garden: Choosing the Perfect Location and Containers. *The Green Cities*. April 17th, 2017. Online.

https://www.thegreencities.com/lifestyle/start-container-garden-choosing-perfect-location-containers/

Gardenuity. 2020. How to Pick the Best Location for a Container Garden. *Gardenuity*. 10th July 2020. Online. https://blog.gardenuity.com/best-location-container-garden/

Kevin. 2022. Best Location for Container Gardening: 4 Clear-Cut Steps. *Gardening Mentor.* Online. https://gardeningmentor.com/best-location-for-container-gardening/

Container Gardening Equipment

Cool Garden. 2015. Basic Equipment for a Container Garden. *Cool Garden.* 21st Feb 2015. Online. https://www.coolgarden.me/basic-equipment-for-a-container-garden-3185/

Garden Design

Balcony Garden Web. 2021. 11 Most Essential Container Garden Design Tips – Designing a Container Garden. *Balcony Garden Web.* Online.

https://balconygardenweb.com/container-garden-design-tips-designing-a-container-garden/

Balcony Garden Web. 2017. 22 Stunning Container Vegetable Garden Design Ideas & Tips. *Balcony Garden Web.* Online. https://balconygardenweb.com/container-vegetable-garden-design-ideas-tips/

Growing Medium

Andrychowicz, Amy. N.d. Choosing the Best Potting Soil Mix for Container Gardening. *Get Busy Gardening.* Online. https://getbusygardening.com/potting-soil-for-container-gardening/

Barnett, Tonya. 2022. Outdoor Potting Soil – Making a Container Growing Medium. *Gardening Know How.* Online. https://www.gardeningknowhow.com/special/containers/potting-soil-for-outdoor-containers.htm

Gonzalez, Ramon. 2018. Test Your Potting Soil Quality Before Planting Your Container Garden. 11th October 2018. Online. *Treehugger.* https://www.treehugger.com/test-your-potting-soil-quality-soil-planting-your-container-garden-4857230

Loughrey, Janet. 2022. Potting Soil 101: Find the Right Mix. *Garden Design.* Online. https://www.gardendesign.com/how-to/potting-soil.html

Reich, Lee. N.d. Soil in Containers Should be a Good Mix. *Fine Gardening.* Online. https://www.finegardening.com/article/soil-in-containers-should-be-a-good-mix

Shelly. 2022. The Best Soil for Container Gardening. *Frugal Family Home.* Online. https://frugalfamilyhome.com/home/gardening/best-soil-for-container-gardening

Shinn, Meghan. 2017. An Easy Test for Your Container Soil. *Horticulture*. 25th July 2017. Online. https://www.hortmag.com/headline/an-easy-test-for-your-container-soil

University of Illinois Extension. 2022. Successful Container Gardens: Using Soil and Soil Mixes. *University of Illinois Extension*. Online.

https://web.extension.illinois.edu/containergardening/soil.cfm

Starting a Container Garden

Deanna. 2019. Potting up Seedlings: What, Why, When & How. *Homestead and Chill*. March 14 2019. Online. https://homesteadandchill.com/potting-up-seedlings/

Gardener's Supply Company. 2022. How to Start Seeds: A comprehensive guide to growing vegetables and flowers from seed. 15th Feb 2022. Online. *Gardener's Supply Company*. https://www.gardeners.com/how-to/how-to-start-seeds/5062.html

Horti Daily. 2017. Seeds vs. Seedlings: What is Better? *Horti Daily*. Online. https://www.hortidaily.com/article/6032426/seeds-vs-seedlings-what-is-better/

Iannotti, Marie. 2021. Vegetable Seeds or Seedlings? Find Out Which Is Best for Your Garden. *The Spruce*. Online. 20th October 2021. https://www.thespruce.com/vegetable-garden-seeds-or-seedlings-1403412

Johnson, Lee. 2022. What Are the Differences between Seeds and Seedlings? *HomeQuestionsAnswered*. 20th February 2022. Online.

https://www.homequestionsanswered.com/what-are-the-differences-between-seeds-and-seedlings.htm

Naples Botanical Garden. N.d. Container Gardening: Seed Starting 101. *Naples Botanical Garden*. Online. https://www.naplesgarden.org/container-gardening-seed-starting-101/

Neveln, Viveka. 2022. Seed-Starting Essentials Every Gardener Should Know. *Better Homes and Gardens*. 13th January, 2022. Online. https://www.bhg.com/gardening/yard/garden-care/seed-starting-essentials/

Maintaining Your Container Garden

Enjoy Container Gardening. 2022. Container Garden Maintenance. *Enjoy Container Gardening*. Online. https://www.enjoycontainergardening.com/blog/container-garden-maintenance/

Gertz, Lindsey. 2022. Container garden success hinges on proper maintenance. *Total Landscape Care*. 11th March 2022. Online.

https://www.totallandscapecare.com/business/article/15065112/proper-maintenance-for-container-garden-success

National Gardening Association Editors. 2022. Maintaining Container Gardens. *Garden.org*. Online. https://garden.org/learn/articles/view/1277/

Savvy Gardening. 2022. Container Garden Maintenance Tips: Help Your Plants Thrive All Summer Long. Online. *Savvy Gardening*. https://savvygardening.com/container-garden-maintenance-tips/

Smith, Mark Ridsdill. 2014. A Guide to Watering Your Container Garden. *The Guardian*. Online. 18th July 2014. https://www.theguardian.com/lifeandstyle/2014/jul/18/guide-watering-container-garden

University of Illinois Extension. 2022. Successful Container Gardens: Watering. *University of Illinois Extension*. Online. https://web.extension.illinois.edu/containergardening/watering.cfm

Harvesting and Storing Vegetables, Fruits, and Herbs

Bradbury, Kate. 2010. Storing and Preserving Your Garden Harvest. *GrowVeg*. Online. https://www.growveg.com/guides/storing-and-preserving-your-garden-harvest/

Naples Botanical Garden. N. d. Container Gardening: General Harvesting Guidelines. *Naples Botanical Garden*. Online. https://www.naplesgarden.org/container-gardening-general-harvesting-guidelines/

University of Florida. 2021. Harvest as You Grow Container Gardening. *Gardening Solutions*. Online. https://gardeningsolutions.ifas.ufl.edu/design/types-of-gardens/havest-as-you-grow-container.html

General Information on Container Gardening

Good House Keeping. 2018. Everything you Need to Know About Container Gardening. *Good House Keeping*. 13th August, 2018. Online. https://www.goodhousekeeping.com/home/gardening/a20707074/container-gardening-tips/

Pierson, Barb. 2018. Harvest Fresh Fruits and Vegetables from Pots on Your Patio. *White Flower Farm*. 1st June 2018. Online. https://www.whiteflowerfarm.com/blog/2018/06/01/harvest-fresh-fruits-vegetables-from-pots-on-your-patio/

Will, Melissa J. 2021. How to Grow Vegetables in Containers From Spring to Fall. *Empress of Dirt*. 18th November 2021. Online. https://empressofdirt.net/growing-veggies-containers/

Pest Control

Almanac. 2022. Fungus Gnats. *Almanac*. Online. https://www.almanac.com/pest/fungus-gnats

Baessler, Liz. 2022. Container Garden Pest Control – Dealing With Pests In Containers. 22nd March 2022. Online. *Gardening Know How*. https://www.gardeningknowhow.com/special/containers/container-pests.htm

Balcony Container Gardening. 2018. 5 Tips for Aphid Control. *Balcony Container Gardening*. Online. http://www.balconycontainergardening.com/wildlife/633-tips-for-aphid-control

BBC Gardeners' World Magazine. 2019. Leaf Miner Fly. *Gardeners' World*. Online. https://www.gardenersworld.com/how-to/solve-problems/leaf-miner-fly/

BBC Gardeners' World Magazine. 2021. Thrips. *Gardeners' World*. Online. https://www.gardenersworld.com/how-to/solve-problems/thrips/

Carroll, Jackie. 2022. Ants in Flower Pots: How to Get Rid of Ants in Pots. *Gardening Know How*. Online. 22nd March 2022. https://www.gardeningknowhow.com/plant-problems/pests/insects/ants-in-flower-pots.htm

Kevin. 2022. How to Get Rid of Pill Bugs in Potted Plants (12 Organic Ways). *Gardening Mentor*. Online. https://gardeningmentor.com/how-to-get-rid-of-pill-bugs-in-potted-plants/

Loughrey, Janet. 2022. How to Identify and Control Spider Mites on Plants. *Garden Design*. Online. https://www.gardendesign.com/how-to/spider-mites.html

Naples Botanical Garden. N.d. Container Gardening: Bugs: Friends or Foes? *Naples Botanical Garden*. Online. https://www.naplesgarden.org/container-gardening-bugs-friends-or-foes/

Planet Natural Research Center. 2022. Springtail. *Planet Natural Research Center*. Online. https://www.planetnatural.com/pest-problem-solver/houseplant-pests/springtail-control/

Dealing with Diseases

Enjoy Container Gardening. 2022. Disease in Container Gardens. *Enjoy Container Gardening*. Online. https://www.enjoycontainergardening.com/blog/disease-in-container-gardens/

Nutrient Deficiencies

Down, Alan. 2019. Common Nutrient Deficiencies or Plants. 5th December 2019. Online. *Down to Earth*. https://down-to-earth.co.uk/soils/common-nutrient-deficiencies-of-plants/

Plant Profiles

Almanac. 2022. Growing Guides. *Almanac*. Online. https://www.almanac.com/gardening/growing-guides

BBC Gardeners' World Magazine. 2020. How to Grow Plants. *Gardener's World*. Online. https://www.gardenersworld.com/how-to/grow-plants/

Garden Design. 2022. 21 Easy Flowers for Beginners to Grow *Garden Design*. Online. https://www.gardendesign.com/flowers/easy.html

Hagen, Linda. 2022. Grow Marigolds for No Fuss Color in the Garden. *Garden Design*. Online. https://www.gardendesign.com/flowers/marigold.html

Iannotti, Marie. 2021. Nasturtium Plant Profile. *The Spruce*. Online. 27th January 2021. https://www.thespruce.com/nasturtiums-cool-season-flowers-1402910

The Spruce. 2022. Plants & Flowers. *The Spruce*. Online. https://www.thespruce.com/plants-and-flowers-5092674

Noyes, Amber. 2021. The 15 Best Vegetables to Grow in Pots and Containers. *Gardening Chores*. Online. 28th April 2021. https://www.gardeningchores.com/best-vegetables-to-grow-in-pots/

Index

Made in the USA
Las Vegas, NV
17 March 2023

69185966R00116